Studies in the History of American Labor

Edited by
Stuart Bruchey
Allan Nevins Professor Emeritus
Columbia University

A Routledge Series

A Strategic Model of
Temporary Staffing

Kay McGlashan Glasgow

Routledge
New York & London / 2001

Published in 2001 by
Routledge
29 West 35th Street
New York, NY 10001

Routledge is an imprint of the Taylor & Francis Group
Printed in the United States of America on acid-free paper.

10 9 8 7 6 5 4 3 2 1

Library of Congress Cataloging-in-Publication Data

Cataloging-in-Publication data is available from the Library of Congress.

ISBN 0-8153-3731-0

DEDICATION

This book is dedicated to my husband Doug,

and to my parents Mary Ellen Lawrence and Bob McGlashan.

Thanks for everything!

Contents

List of Figures

List of Tables

Acknowledgments

This study was funded in part by a grant from the SHRM Foundation. The interpretations, conclusions, and recommendations, however, are those of the author and do not necessarily reflect those of the Foundation.

I would like to acknowledge several people who were instrumental in helping me finish my dissertation, upon which this book is based. My dissertation committee, consisting of Pat Wright, Ricky Griffin, Lynda Kilbourne, and Mary Zey, provided guidance and helpful feedback. Jay Dial, Amy Hillman, Karen Jansen, Gerry Keim and Ann McFadyen provided valuable insight and moral support. The management faculty at Texas A&M University, especially Don Hellriegel and Dick Woodman, provided me with a professional and supportive working environment during my graduate studies and this research project. The faculty of the College of Business at Cal Poly State University, San Luis Obispo, particularly Rebecca Ellis, Jim Sena, Rami Shani, and Mike Stebbins, continued this support while I completed my project.

All of my parents, Bob and Nina McGlashan, and Mary Ellen and John Lawrence, were a source of inspiration for me. My father, Bob, shared helpful advice and support during the research process. My mother, Mary Ellen, was particularly instrumental in encouraging me to complete my work. And my husband, Doug Glasgow, provided constant support, love, and belief in me.

KMG

CHAPTER ONE

Introduction

A recent trend in the study of human resource management is the linking of human resource practices to the strategic imperatives of the firm. This new area of interest has been labeled "Strategic Human Resource Management," or SHRM (Butler, Ferris and Napier, 1991; Cappelli and Singh, 1992; Tichy, Fombrun and Devanna, 1982). Wright and McMahan (1992: 298) define SHRM as "the pattern of planned human resource deployments and activities intended to enable an organization to achieve its goals." SHRM is concerned with the design and implementation of human resource practices and programs that promote strategy-consistent behaviors on the part of the firm's human assets. Strategy-consistent behavior by employees is purported to improve the strategic effectiveness of the firm as a whole (Jackson, Schuler, and Rivero, 1989; Snell, 1992). Strategic effectiveness means that an organization is more proficient in achieving its strategic goals, which may then translate into higher shareholder returns. In addition, the integration of the various HR functions into the overall strategic plan of the organization is also contended to be beneficial in that human resource capabilities are considered during strategy formulation and implementation.

One of the criticisms of SHRM research is that it has not taken adequate advantage of existing macro organization theories in order to empirically test strategic human resource activities (Wright and McMahan, 1992). SHRM research is more often theoretical than empirical in nature, and it has also typically been limited in its use of existing organizational research. SHRM literature has been developed at the individual human resource practice level as well as by examining the interrelationships among the practices. Both types of research are important at this early stage of SHRM theory development. SHRM researchers would further benefit from development of comprehensive testable models at both the individual practice and overall HR pattern levels, using established macro level literature from the areas of organizational strategy and organization theory, in order to integrate strategic human resource management into a more coherent whole.

In this book, I examine a particular aspect of the human resource function, that of staffing decisions regarding hiring arrangements with employees. A recent heightened interest in "contingent" (e.g., temporary or contract) employment arrangements makes the issue of permanent versus temporary labor a timely one. Organizations are increasingly using contingent labor to deal with the present economic environment (Cooper, 1995; Houseman, 1999; Kahn and Foulkes, 1995; Mangum, Mayall and Nelson, 1985; Pfeffer and Baron, 1988; Rousseau and Wade-Benzoni, 1995; Segal and Sullivan, 1995). Many firms are turning to contingent, contract, and temporary workers instead of permanent full-time employees in order to be more "competitive" and "flexible" in their staffing levels (Abraham, 1988; Kahn and Foulkes, 1995; Khojasteh, 1994; Pfeffer and Baron, 1988; Segal and Sullivan, 1995; SHRM, 1998). Contemporary firms are utilizing contingent staffing arrangements so as to cut costs (e.g., fewer or no benefits, perception of decreased potential litigation, decreased overhead) as well as to survive fluctuations in product demand. Contingent labor can theoretically offer these cost savings, as long as the work contract can be specified such that it assures the tasks will be accomplished to a firm's desired standards at its desired costs.

In spite of these trends, the decision to either internalize an employee or contract in the market for the work is one that has not received much attention in the SHRM literature. The majority of previous strategic staffing research has taken for granted that a permanent hire will occur. Most of this research is limited to managerial positions. Researchers have explored areas such as matching managerial characteristics to environmental contingencies (Gupta and Govindarajan, 1984; Guthrie, Grimm, and Smith, 1991); designing the staffing process according to strategic contingencies (Sonnenfeld and Peiperl, 1988; Cohen and Pfeffer, 1986; Guthrie and Olian, 1991); deciding whether to develop managerial skills internally or hire from the outside (Kerr and Jackofsky, 1989); and the role of strategy as a moderator between human resource skills and organizational performance (Wright, Smart, and McMahan, 1995).

The initial decision whether to make the employment relationship a temporary or permanent one has been largely ignored (Davis-Blake and Uzzi, 1993; Kahn and Foulkes, 1995; Pfeffer and Baron, 1988). Furthermore, no research exists investigating the use of permanent or temporary employees from a strategic perspective. The purpose of this book is to utilize Porter's (1980) strategy typology and transaction cost (Williamson, 1975, 1985) literature to develop a theoretical model of a firm's permanent staffing needs based on the influence of strategy on transaction costs in the employment relationship. We can then make predictions based on a firm's chosen business strategy (Porter, 1980) regarding the appropriate usage of temporary employment both overall and within particular job categories. If used appropriately, temporary employment is then purported to lead to improved organizational performance.

Chapter two presents a discussion of contingent employment, including its importance in today's organizations, its benefits and costs. In chapter three, Porter's (1980) generic competitive strategy typology is described and then integrated with transaction cost theory (Williamson, 1975, 1985) and supporting organizational theories to develop a strategic model of temporary employment. Chapter four introduces hypotheses to be tested in the study. In chapter five, the research methodology is described, including description of the research survey and variable operationalizations. Results are presented in chapter six. Chapter seven concludes the book with a discussion of the study's findings, limitations, directions for future research and conclusions.

I now turn to a more in-depth discussion of the temporary employment phenomenon. Chapter two examines the contingent employment setting in more detail. First, contingent employment is defined. The nature of today's work force and the specific role of contingent employment are also discussed. Next, benefits and costs of contingent employment that have been cited in previous literature will be reviewed. Third, the overall use of temporary employment within firms will be discussed, introducing its linkage to Porter's competitive strategies and to transaction cost theory.

CHAPTER TWO

The Nature of Contingent Employment

CONTINGENT EMPLOYMENT AND THE NATURE OF TODAY'S WORK FORCE

The contingent workforce has become a vital part of the modern organizational world. The term "contingent" has recently been criticized for being too broad (Cooper, 1995; Houseman, 1999; Polivka and Nardone, 1989; Segal and Sullivan, 1995). Contingent employment historically has conjured up the impression of the "Kelly Girl" or female clerical worker. This is no longer a valid impression, as contingent workers enjoy a variety of employment arrangements (Cooper, 1995; Micco, 1999) in a multiplicity of jobs and fields, including administrative and support, technical, managerial, health and computer related employment (Kahn and Foulkes, 1995; Segal and Sullivan, 1995). The pool of contingent workers is also diverse in terms of gender, race, education and work experience (Segal and Sullivan, 1995).

Cooper (1995) provides seven general categories of the contingent workforce. First, **temporary employees** typically work for one employer for a short period of time and then move on to another organization in a similar capacity. Second, **part-time employees** are those employees with abbreviated hours that carry on job functions similar to others in the organization. Third, **seasonal employees** are used during upswings in business cycles. Fourth, **independent contractors** are those who provide a particular service or skill for a prenegotiated price, usually offsite from the contracting employer. Fifth, **leased employees** are those employees who are contracted for through a third party to carry out many of the administrative tasks for the contracting organization, although the leased employees usually perform work at the client's site. Sixth, **involuntary self-employed individuals** are classified as part of the contingent workforce when they are performing functions such as contracting and consulting. Last, **casual employees** are normally part of collective bargaining agreements between organizations and unions. They represent a reserve that organizations under such agreements are obligated to use in times when regular employees are unavailable or during times of business necessity.

Each of these classifications of contingent workers will have different employment arrangements with contracting organizations. This introduces difficulties into the discussion and the examination of contingent employment. Researchers should take care to distinguish among these arrangements when investigating the causes and effects of contingent employment. For instance, Davis-Blake and Uzzi (1993) found different determinants of employment externalization for temporary workers and independent contractors. Segal and Sullivan (1995) examined the make-up of the temporary labor force, and they found that wage differentials between temporary and permanent workers varied among white, pink, and blue collar positions. Thus, we must be more specific about the type of contingent arrangement when drawing conclusions about temporary work. A single research study cannot possibly encompass all of these employment arrangements. Therefore, I limit the scope of the study to the first classification listed above, that of temporary employees, to avoid confounding of different employment arrangements. Future research should, of course, examine each of the different classifications.

As previously mentioned, existing staffing research carries the assumption that a permanent hire will occur and then examines variables such as relevant managerial characteristics or components of the staffing procedure. This hiring assumption may no longer be entirely valid or appropriate for the current employment climate (Pfeffer and Baron, 1988). Firms are increasingly utilizing the services of contingent employees in various organizational capacities (Cooper, 1995; Davis-Blake and Uzzi, 1993; Mangum et al., 1985; Micco, 1999; Pearce, 1993; Segal and Sullivan, 1995). A "dual labor market" of sorts is now characterized in the organizational literature, made up of a "core" or "permanent" workforce on the one hand and a "contingent" or "buffer" workforce on the other (Mangum et al., 1985; Pfeffer and Baron, 1988). Recent estimates of the percentage of workers who are in contingent arrangements have ranged from about four to thirty percent of the labor force, depending on the source of the data and the definition of contingent work used (Caudron, 1994a; Bureau of Labor Statistics, 1999; Houseman, 1999; Belous, 1989). In response to "overly broad estimates" by some researchers in the 1980s and 1990s, the Bureau of Labor Statistics (BLS) began a survey program in 1995 to more accurately measure contingent work arrangements (Houseman, 1999; Polivka and Nardone, 1989). According to the BLS, the percentage of workers who classified themselves as contingent (i.e., did not expect their jobs to last for economic reasons) in 1999 was 4.3 percent (BLS, 1999).

In general, the core workforce is provided with more established internal job ladders (Baron, Davis-Blake and Bielby, 1986), more job security, higher levels of employee development (Mangum et al., 1985), greater benefits (Mangum et al., 1985), and a more mutually obligatory psychological contract (Rousseau and Parks, 1993). These core workers typically have skills that are essential to fulfilling customer demand and that are not readily available on the open market (Baron et al., 1986; Mangum et al., 1985).

Contingent workers, in contrast, tend to have more generic skills that can be applied in numerous organizations (Mangum et al., 1985). They typically receive little job security, have no established opportunities for advancement, and have been shown to form a more transactional (e.g., short-term, non-relational) type of psychological contract with employing organizations (Pfeffer and Baron, 1988; Rousseau and Parks, 1993; Rousseau and Wade-Benzoni, 1995).

Many reasons are cited by employers for use of contingent employment. Temporary employees may possibly be less expensive and may offer flexibility in staffing levels. The benefits and costs of contingent usage are explored in the next section.

BENEFITS AND COSTS OF CONTINGENT EMPLOYMENT

Certain legal, institutional, and external competitive pressures as well as possible labor cost savings have been cited as probable reasons for the increased use of contingent work arrangements (Abraham, 1988; Houseman, 1999; Mangum et al., 1985; Pearce, 1993; Pfeffer and Baron, 1988). Increased litigation in the areas of employment discrimination and wrongful discharge, for example, has caused some employers to avoid permanent employment as a means of reducing the risk of such lawsuits (Autor, 2000; Cooper, 1995; Pearce, 1993). Institutional factors have also given rise to greater numbers of contingent workers. One such factor may be management limiting "head counts" of permanent employees and yet at the same time allowing for hiring contractors. Another possible factor is the presence of unions restricting permanent employment arrangements such that hiring temporaries may be more cost-efficient and flexible than hiring workers that are covered by collective bargaining agreements (Pearce, 1993). Increased global competition has made it imperative for U.S. organizations to reduce costs as much as possible and do "more with less" in terms of employees (Pearce, 1993; Pfeffer and Baron, 1988). Increased competition combined with changing consumer tastes that are requiring more variety (and thus specialization in production) are driving the need for cost savings (Pfeffer and Baron, 1988).

Labor cost savings in contingent employment use may accrue to organizations in the areas of benefits, wages, recruitment, selection, training, and organizational exit (Autor, 2000; Cooper, 1995; Herer and Harel, 1998; Houseman, 1999; Pfeffer and Baron, 1988; Segal and Sullivan, 1995).

ingent workers historically receive few to no benefits from employing organizations, and their wages are typically lower than those of permanent workers (Cooper, 1995; Mangum et al., 1985; Segal and Sullivan, 1995). Recruitment and selection costs are reduced as contingent workers are often hired through agencies that incur these costs as well as some training costs (Mangum et al., 1985). Although temporary agencies typically charge a premium in return for such trained employees, it appears that overall wage costs still stay below that of permanent workers, especially due to benefits savings (Segal and Sullivan, 1995). However, salary savings may be minimal (Kahn and Foulkes, 1995). Firms may also ultimately hire contingent workers full-time without having had incurred search costs and after the opportunity to preview workers' performance, thus lowering selection costs (Segal and Sullivan, 1995).

Staff reduction costs such as severance pay may also be reduced, as contingent workers are hired with the understanding that their work may be terminated after a short time (Autor, 2000; Mangum et al., 1985). This introduces the concept of flexibility into organizational staffing (Abraham, 1988; Cooper, 1995; Mangum et al., 1985; Pearce, 1993; Pfeffer and Baron, 1988; Segal and Sullivan, 1995). Organizations that experience cyclical or unstable demand for their products or services tend to utilize contingent employees in periods of higher demand. This allows firms to easily adjust employment levels. Uncertainty about the external market may in fact be reduced in this manner, as organizations can adjust quickly and with relative ease to such fluctuations. Indeed, in interviews conducted with a small number of top level human resource managers, Kahn and Foulkes (1995) found that managers cited staffing flexibility as a key reason for using temporary employees more often than citing labor cost savings. These managers feel that benefits accrue from not hiring regular employees in turbulent times.

In addition to the above potential organizational benefits of contingent employment, limitations also exist. First, it is recognized that contingent workers are not appropriate for all jobs, especially not for those positions that involve the use of firm-specific skills and knowledge (Abraham, 1988; Autor, 2000; Mangum et al., 1985; Pearce, 1993; Pfeffer, 1994; Williamson, 1985). Workers who enter a firm temporarily may have neither the opportunity nor the inclination to develop firm-specific skills or knowledge. Permanent employees are likely a better choice in jobs that involve firm-idiosyncratic knowledge and skills, such as customer relations (Pfeffer, 1994), management positions (Pfeffer and Baron, 1988), or jobs with high technical and informational complexity (Davis-Blake and Uzzi, 1993; Rousseau and Wade-Benzoni, 1995). Permanent employees are better suited to such jobs because they tend to benefit from developing knowledge and skills that in turn makes the organization more dependent on their continued employment (Robinson, Kraatz and Rousseau, 1994).

Relational contracts tend to develop when employees and organizations come to rely upon one another, such that the parties develop reciprocal obligations. In return for developing firm-specific capabilities, employees expect to receive benefits such as long-term employment and advancement opportunities (Autor, 2000; Robinson et al., 1994).

Research into the benefits and costs of contingent employment is sparse, with most literature consisting of theory and assertions rather than empirical evidence. Most agree that wage and benefit expenses are indeed lower for contingent employees (Pfeffer and Baron, 1988). A widely cited level is that contingent hourly wage rates and benefits are about three-quarters of permanent employee levels (Segal and Sullivan, 1995). A major difficulty in determining wage differentials, however, may be related to the data that currently exists. Most national level data is in the aggregate, which mixes together temporary, contract, leased and other contingent employees of varying experience and task levels. No national studies exist comparing the costs and returns of contingent workers with permanent employees at the firm or job level, so this cost savings may be questionable (Caudron, 1994b). Organization-level data at the very least, and job-level data at best, are needed to establish wage savings in the future.

Empirical research regarding the impact of inappropriately using temporary employment is also limited. It is generally agreed that temporaries are not appropriate when firm-specific knowledge is necessary, as previously noted, or when the outcomes of employee performance are vitally important. In an empirical analysis of industry data and court-imposed limitations on employment-at-will, Autor (2000) suggested that the tremendous growth of the temporary help supply services industry sector over the past twenty years has been due to organizations outsourcing positions with the lowest required firm-specific skills. It may be that job performance of temporary employees is different from that of permanent employees in terms of effort, dedication, and performance level, for example, and this may have an important impact on organizational outcomes (Nollen and Axel, 1996). Furthermore, different organizational settings may be more or less appropriate for using temporary employees.

Whether or not economic benefit to the organization exists in terms of labor cost savings due to use of temporary employees is an important empirical question for future research to address. It is not, however, the focus of this research study. Assuming that firms will indeed realize some sort of labor cost savings or other economic benefit in using temporary employees if done so appropriately, we may then take the next step in developing a strategic model of temporary staffing in this study. The union of competitive strategy and transaction cost theory aids us in predicting under which strategies temporary employees may be more or less appropriate. A discussion of this theoretical consolidation follows in chapter three.

Temporary Staffing and Competitive Strategy

The previous discussion in chapter two emphasizes our lack of knowledge regarding contingent employment in general and temporary employment in particular. Consistent empirical evidence does not yet exist to show that temporary labor is indeed cost effective in all cases. Furthermore, we know very little about the link of firm and job characteristics to effective use of temporary employees. In developing a strategic model of temporary employment, we must consider the strategic aspect of temporary employee usage. The setting in which temporary employees operate may affect the strategic effectiveness of organizations.

In this chapter, the competitive strategy typology developed by Porter (1980) is introduced. Then, in order to make assertions regarding the effect of strategic choice on staffing decisions, we must integrate strategy with transaction cost theory and supporting organizational theories in order to make predictions regarding the nature of the employment relationship.

PORTER'S COMPETITIVE STRATEGY FRAMEWORK

Several different typologies of organizational and competitive strategies exist in the strategic management literature (Miles and Snow, 1978; Porter, 1980). One typology that has been utilized often in human resource literature is that of cost leadership, differentiation, and focus introduced by Porter (1980; Arthur, 1992; Guthrie and Olian, 1991). These competitive strategies have been found to impact and be impacted by human resource activities in organizations.

Porter (1980) found these competitive strategies to be followed by many firms in order to deal with competitive forces. He suggested that three generic business-level strategies exist: cost leadership, differentiation, and focus. A cost leadership strategy is one in which a firm's major focus is on providing a product or service at the cheapest price (Porter, 1980). Firms following a cost leadership strategy gain competitive advantage by being mass producers of sorts, attempting to gain the greatest market share possible through economies of scale and by making products more cheaply.

Firms may instead follow a differentiation strategy, in which they attempt to set themselves apart from other organizations by offering a unique product or service (Porter, 1980). In exchange for this uniqueness, consumers will theoretically pay a higher price for the product or service. Competitive advantage is not gained through increased market share, but through a smaller loyal customer following that is willing to pay higher prices for differentiated products.

The focus strategy is one in which firms concentrate on particular segments of their markets (Porter, 1980). Focus firms may be either cost leaders or differentiators. The difference is that these firms focus on a particular buyer group, product line segment or geographic market, with the intent of serving the focused segment very well, either through lower prices or differentiated products or services (Porter, 1980). Alternatively, firms may use a breadth strategy, in which they market to the broadest market possible.

STRATEGY AND HUMAN RESOURCE MANAGEMENT

Porter's (1980) generic strategies have been verified through empirical research. Further, they have been previously utilized in human resource management literature (e.g., Arthur, 1992; Guthrie and Olian, 1991). In the field of SHRM, recent research conducted by Arthur (1992, 1994) is widely cited as an example of demonstrating the interface between competitive business level strategy and human resource activities. In a study of steel mini-mills, Arthur (1992) found that competitive strategy (either cost leadership or differentiation) was significantly associated with the type of industrial relations (IR) system used. These mills exhibited one of two general IR systems, control or commitment (Arthur, 1994). Control IR systems were typified by low wages, low-skilled jobs, little employee participation in decision-making – i.e., the types of HR activities one would associate with a firm following a cost leadership competitive strategy. Those mills classified as having commitment IR systems, on the other hand, exhibited HR practices including highly skilled jobs, higher wages and more employee participation in decision-making. These practices were significantly associated with mills following a differentiation strategy. Such HR practices are designed to develop a commitment between employees and the employer.

Arthur's work shows that a firm's strategy and its HR activities are highly interrelated. The issue of staffing choice (i.e., permanent or temporary) was not explicitly addressed in his research, but Arthur's results lend support to the notion here that strategy has a strong effect on the decisions of HR managers in choosing appropriate HR policies and practices.

Extending the control versus commitment approach, we se(this book. Control HR systems are designed to control th employees in mechanized, low-skill settings (Arthur, 1992). commitment is developed between the employee and emplo, ... ⊥ ⅠⅠⅠⅠⅠⅠ ⅠS exactly the type of setting in which temporary employees may provide an attractive alternative to permanent employees. In commitment HR settings, employers use HR practices designed to keep employees with their organizations by providing higher wages, greater participation, more extensive training and self-managing teams (Arthur, 1992). In general, these types of HR activities may not be cost effective in the temporary employment situation but instead would be better suited to the permanent employment arrangement.

Particularly in integrated manufacturing settings, it appears that higher skills are required of employees to carry out tasks when utilizing advanced manufacturing technology, total quality management, or just-in-time manufacturing. These types of manufacturing systems may be considered ways to establish differentiation as a competitive strategy. Arthur (1992) has shown that commitment HR activities are more effective in integrated manufacturing settings. Employees in these settings are expected to take initiative and responsibility in such settings. In return, the employees receive more training, rewards for strategy-consistent performance, and longer term contracts. This is the exact situation in which permanent employees are best utilized.

Conversely, cost leadership manufacturing settings, where automation and economies of scale are key, would reflect control mechanisms in their HR systems rather than commitment mechanisms. Such firms would not benefit from extensive training of temporaries, as these employees will not work for the organization on a long-term basis. Participation and self-management by temporaries will also not be effective, as temporary employees will not likely be motivated to work toward organizational goals without supervision by others. These temporary employees would have little to gain by doing so. Thus, it appears that Arthur's (1992) research will lend some support to the ideas presented within this book.

Another stream of research by Snell and Dean (1992; Snell, 1992; Dean and Snell, 1991) contributes additional complementary support to the study. In this research, the issue of "control" in HR activities is explicitly addressed. Based on the amount of knowledge that managers have about cause-effect relationships and standards of desirable performance, they can use the type of control system most appropriate to their needs. The control system is used to encourage employees to behave in an optimal fashion based on organizational context.

Within this context, jobs will have varying degrees to which their tasks may be programmed and their job performance readily observed (Snell and Dean, 1992; Eisenhardt, 1989). Behavioral controls, which include close monitoring and structured tasks, may be used in more easily observable performance jobs in which the cause-effect relationship between tasks and outcomes is well understood. However, as jobs become less programmable and/or performance less observable, behavioral controls become less effective while output or input controls become more effective.

Output controls use decentralized discretion pushed down to the employee level (i.e., high autonomy) with performance outcomes serving as the basis for evaluation rather than behaviors, as effective behaviors are not easily identified. When ambiguity exists in both cause-effect relationships and performance standards, input control is most appropriate. In this scenario, heavy reliance is placed on rigorous staffing procedures, training and socialization in order for employees to act in the firm's best interest (Snell and Dean, 1992; Ouchi, 1980).

The control theory research also lends support to our model of temporary staffing. As behavior controls are generally used in more programmable positions, temporary employees can be used effectively in that managers can observe whether temporaries are doing what they have been hired to do. However, as the job situation becomes more ambiguous in terms of cause-effect relationships and performance observability, it is less likely that temps will be utilized. The autonomous nature of jobs under output and input control systems make them poor candidates for the temporary employment arrangement. Particularly in the case of input controls, rigorous staffing, training and socialization will likely make permanent arrangements more effective. In any case, the nature of jobs within a firm is affected by its chosen competitive strategy. Strategy then affects the choice of control mechanisms that are most effective under strategic contingencies.

Both Arthur's and Snell and Dean's research relies heavily on the theory of human capital espoused by Becker (1962). In general, human capital theory suggests that the knowledge, skills and abilities of people can provide economic value to a firm (Becker, 1962). Firms invest in firm-specific training of their human capital in hopes that future economic gains will result from employees' capabilities and effort. Employees who receive training from their organizations expect in return to be rewarded for applying their capabilities, especially those capabilities that are firm-specific. Rewards include additional training, compensation and long term job contracts (Becker, 1962). Turnover can be particularly costly to organizations if training outlays are extensive. The firm is therefore encouraged to enter into long-term contracts in order to receive a return on its investment.

Especially in the case of more "specialized" strategies, human capital investment appears to be extremely important in realizing performance gains under such strategies. Regarding specialized strategies such as differentiation (Arthur, 1992), advanced manufacturing technology (Snell and Dean, 1992), and quality (Youndt, Snell, Dean and Lepak, 1996), authors have virtually unanimously claimed that human capital provides the key to successful implementation of these strategies.

Firms need to recoup the expenditures from activities such as on-the-job training, education and developmental opportunities, which are considered to increase human capital within a firm. Otherwise, the expenditures become worthless. Therefore, we would not expect to find extensive training or education offered to temporary employees. This would run counter to Becker's (1962) theory. Referring to Arthur's and Snell and Dean's work, the use of a commitment HR system or an input control system necessarily results in greater investments in a firm's human capital. We can infer that commitment HR systems and input control systems are geared toward the permanent employment arrangement simply because these systems are based on receiving a return on investment in human capital. Moreover, these types of systems are closely tied to organizational context, namely competitive strategy.

With these theories to support our idea that strategy and HR staffing are intertwined, it seems appropriate to invoke Porter's (1980) typology to test our assertions about temporary staffing. However, recent criticisms have arisen in the use of the Porter typology in SHRM research (Chadwick and Cappelli, 1999). One criticism is that the complexity of HR systems within organizations makes it difficult to establish empirical relationships between HR practices and firm typologies. Further, the typologies themselves are said to be overly simplistic operationalizations of strategy which cannot capture the richness of strategic actions (Chadwick and Cappelli, 1999).

A more recent conceptualization of strategy is as a firm's search for "competitive advantage," i.e., the resource-based view of the firm (Barney, 1991). A firm will identify idiosyncratic value-creating activities it carries out that are rare and that other organizations cannot imitate. Thus, an organization can realize strategic goals in countless ways, not just by choosing cost leadership or differentiation. Additionally, "pure types" (i.e., strictly cost leadership or differentiation) of Porter's competitive strategies are rare (Chadwick and Cappelli, 1999). Therefore, some purport that the use of typologies in strategic management research is obsolete.

One cannot deny that difficulties exist whenever a typology is invoked in organizational research. Any attempt to simplify the world necessarily results in a loss of richness in understanding. However, the appeal to cease use of strategic typologies is in itself overly restrictive. As researchers, we recognize the need for all types of research. It is true that organizations are extremely complex institutions that require in-depth study when plausible. However, the use of broad-based quantitative studies that do try to simplify the organizational world by modeling it and making generalizations about it is equally valuable. Therefore, the use of typologies in SHRM research should be viewed as complementing other research strategies, not replacing them.

Furthermore, the abundance of research supporting the existence of Porter's competitive strategy typology cannot be ignored. Arguably, attempts to classify organizations into "pure" categories of cost leadership, differentiation, focus or breadth is overly restrictive. A continuum of strategic "inclination" may be used, however, that not only mitigates the problem of strict classification but also lends itself more readily to regression analysis. This recognizes that "degrees" of cost leadership, differentiation and focus can exist. This approach is used in the present study.

It is felt to be justifiable, then, to utilize Porter's strategic typology in this research study as, at the very least, an initial attempt to link strategy with temporary staffing. In this study, I attempt to establish linkages between these types of strategies and the type of employment arrangement to utilize (temporary or permanent) in order to sustain competitive advantage. This strategic aspect of temporary staffing has not been previously examined. In order to do so, transaction cost theory is used to link strategy with temporary staffing.

TRANSACTION COST THEORY

In particular, the competitive strategy (Porter, 1980) that an organization chooses may impact the effectiveness of using temporary employees, as it will affect the nature of jobs within the firm. One view from which to analyze the effect of competitive strategy on the nature of jobs is that of transaction cost theory. This theory provides guidelines to help predict when an organization may internalize particular job functions or contract for them in the temporary market under particular competitive strategies. Proper use of employee arrangements may optimize strategic effectiveness, which in transaction cost terms is defined as minimization of transaction costs and subsequent maximization of economic firm performance.

Transaction cost theory seeks to economically explain firm structure in terms of cost minimization of particular employment contractual arrangements by using either the market or hierarchy (Coase, 1937; Alchian and Demsetz, 1972; Williamson, 1979; Williamson and Ouchi, 1981). The organization seeks the most efficient contract (i.e., that minimizes transaction costs) according to attributes of the job, firm and environment (Jones, 1984; Williamson, 1985). The staffing decision may be largely based on information about the nature of work that will be undertaken (e.g., firm-specific activities, ambiguous performance standards, interdependence among employee tasks). This will dictate the type of governance structure necessary to assure that the employee is monitored sufficiently, such that he or she carries out the terms of the employment contract (Jones, 1984; Snell and Dean, 1992).

COMPARISON OF TRANSACTION COST AND AGENCY THEORIES

Transaction cost theory shares several of its assumptions with another organization theory, agency theory (Eisenhardt, 1989; Fama and Jensen, 1983; Jensen and Meckling, 1976). Agency theory also conceptualizes the employment relationship as a contract, and the contract is used to align the goals of organizational principals (i.e., owners or managers) and agents (i.e., employees hired to carry out work on behalf of principals).

Both transaction cost theory and agency theory assume that agents are self-interested and that people have bounded rationality (i.e., limited information capacity). Agent self-interest means that employees will work toward personal rather than organizational goals unless the employment contract encourages them (i.e., controls their behaviors) to work in the firm's best interest. Bounded rationality affects the contracting process itself, in that principals cannot know all consequences of behavior in advance. The employment contract serves as a substitute in the absence of complete information about employee behaviors and performance implications.

Additionally, agency theory assumes that agents have more risk aversion than do principals, because agents cannot diversify their employment risk (Eisenhardt, 1989). Therefore, agents must be encouraged to learn firm-specific skills, for example, by use of the employment contract. Otherwise, the agents would not be willing to assume the risk of having non-transferrable, asset-specific employment skills (Eisenhardt, 1989).

Agency theory espouses the use of either behavior-based or outcome-based contracts as control mechanisms (Eisenhardt, 1989). Behavior-based contracts use salaries and hierarchical governance mechanisms, similar to the use of hierarchy as a control mechanism under the transaction cost framework. Outcome-based contracts involve transfer of property rights and market governance, similar to the use of market-based contracts under transaction cost theory.

However, the two theories differ in two important areas. First, transaction cost theory is concerned with organizational boundaries while agency theory emphasizes the contract itself, regardless of boundary (Eisenhardt, 1989). Second, transaction cost theory examines asset specificity and small numbers bargaining as its independent variables, while agency theory has as independent variables risk attitudes, outcome uncertainty and information systems (Eisenhardt, 1989).

While agency theory certainly complements transaction cost theory, it is not our best choice when examining temporary employment as a market governance mechanism. Our focus is the impact of strategy on jobs within an organization, making temporary employment more or less appropriate. Agency theory does address some job attributes, such as task programmability and outcome uncertainty (i.e., performance ambiguity), but its emphasis is more on the costs of information and differences in risk attitudes. These concepts are similar to those of transaction cost theory, however, and they therefore lend support to the ideas developed in this study.

TRANSACTION COSTS, STRATEGY AND THE STAFFING DECISION

According to SHRM assumptions, the nature of jobs within a firm should be reflective of its competitive strategy. The most critical assumption under transaction cost theory in the area of business strategy is asset specificity, or degree of firm-specific activities required of employees. From human capital theory (Becker, 1962), we know that an employee who develops knowledge and/or skills that are idiosyncratic to a particular firm will develop a more mutually dependent relationship with the organization. The employee's skills and knowledge cannot be readily transferred to another firm setting, so he/she will become more reliant on continued employment with the organization. In return, the employee will become more important to the employing organization.

Transaction cost theory assumes that employees who perform firm-specific activities should be internalized into the firm rather than contracting for the activities in the market. This arrangement would minimize the transaction costs associated with securing the needed activities. The degree of firm-specific activities in an organization is likely contingent on the business strategy chosen by the firm. Transaction cost theory, however, does not address what types of jobs a firm is likely to have. Therefore, in order to make firm-specific hypotheses about the optimal type of employment contract to use, organizational strategy must be integrated with transaction cost theory. Then, the extent of overall temporary employee usage may be hypothesized to differ based on a firm's chosen strategy.

From the standpoint of overall temporary employment, we would expect that a cost leadership strategy would be more consistent with the overall use of temporary employees than would a differentiation strategy. The reasoning stems from the nature of the organizational production systems appropriate for each of the strategies. Cost leaders tend to use mass production and low-skilled employees to create a cost advantage. They commonly invest heavily in capital equipment, design products for ease in manufacturing, and have intense supervision of labor (Porter, 1980). Temporary employees would likely be more appropriate in cost leadership production settings because employees are heavily supervised and are often not expected to be highly or uniquely skilled. Temporaries often fill simplified jobs, are easily trained, and are easily replaced by other employees. High turnover will not likely present a large problem.

Differentiating firms, on the other hand, are expected to create high quality products and services, and require employees with creativity, high skills, and R&D capabilities (Porter, 1980). Many employees are expected to develop firm-specific skills, that is, skills that are only valu employing firm. Permanent employees would have a greater i develop such skills, while temporary employees would gain little from cultivating such expertise. Thus, differentiating firms may have a less appropriate production setting for the temporary employment arrangement on the whole. Furthermore, differentiating firms may gain more from use of long-term permanent employment arrangements than cost leader firms because of increased commitment to the organization and development of idiosyncratic skills.

Market focus may also play a role in the effectiveness of temporary employee usage. A firm that focuses on a narrow market segment will require greater firm-specific skills and knowledge in functions dealing with customer markets in order for employees to better serve the firm's particular customer base. Focus firms are restricting their share of the market and will thus need to serve the fewer clients in a superior fashion through more personalized customer service. Permanent employees are more likely to develop the skills necessary to do this. Employees in particular who deal with marketing activities in firms that restrict their market focus must be superior in analyzing geographic or demographic trends, which may also require higher degrees of firm-specific activities. Thus, market focus may also play a role in strategy-appropriate overall use of temporary employees.

JOB DIFFERENCES AND TEMPORARY EMPLOYEE USAGE

Recognizing that these predictions are at the aggregate firm level, we must also address the topic of specific job attributes that may cause particular jobs to be more or less suitable to temporary employment within a particular firm. A firm with a cost leadership strategy will not be totally comprised of generic, low-skilled jobs. It will necessarily have some jobs that will require firm-specific activities. Similarly, differentiating firms will include jobs with both low and high asset specificity. Breadth and focus marketers will also have jobs that vary in their asset specificity levels. Therefore, it is also important to examine job-level data regarding attributes that make particular positions more or less suitable for temporary employees.

We may visualize Porter's generic strategies as a two-by-two matrix, as in figure 1. We can classify firms as either cost leaders or differentiators on the horizontal axis, and as focus or breadth marketers on the vertical axis. We would expect for those firms in quadrant one that are differentiators with a narrow market focus to require tasks with the highest degree of overall firm-specific capabilities from employees. These firms supply unique products and services to a restricted market segment. Their customers likely expect specialized service and on-going relationships with organizational representatives that have firm-specific knowledge and skills. Conversely, firms with a cost leadership strategy and a broad market focus in quadrant three will likely include a larger percentage of jobs that require the least degree of firm-specific activities. These organizations supply standard products and services to a wide customer base at a low price, and their production processes are standardized in order to create economies of scale.

The remaining two quadrants will probably require a level of firm-specific assets in between the two extremes. That is, production strategy (cost leadership or differentiation) and marketing strategy (breadth or focus) may have different effects on the nature of jobs within organizations. It may be that firm-specific activities within these "mixed" strategy firms vary by job category. Production activities may cause varying degrees of asset specificity in production-related jobs, but may have little to no effect on marketing-related activities. Similarly, the varying focus or breadth of market coverage may necessitate one or more job categories within a firm to carry out more or fewer firm-specific tasks related to marketing efforts. The question that then arises is where the effects of production strategy and marketing strategy will manifest themselves. In other words, do production and marketing strategies have separate effects on jobs within firms based on the responsibilities that the jobs entail? Also, will this affect the levels of temporary employment according to job responsibility?

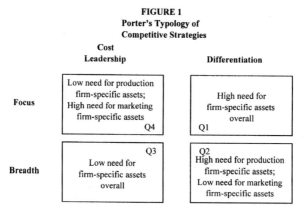

FIGURE 1
Porter's Typology of
Competitive Strategies

Asset specificity levels in manufacturing jobs will be driven by choice of production strategy, namely cost leadership or differentiation. High levels of firm-specific activities in the differentiation production setting will dictate that larger numbers of permanent employees be used in production jobs. Cost leaders, however, may be able to use more temporary employees in production activities because the need for firm-specific activities is minimized by standardization and automation, which simplifies the processes that production workers will carry out.

As firms increasingly focus on narrower markets, they will need to utilize more permanent labor in marketing-oriented positions because of greater asset specificity. Widening the marketing effort, on the other hand, may allow firms to use more temporary labor as marketing activities become more standardized. Thus, we would expect for the effect of competitive marketing strategy to show itself primarily in marketing-related jobs.[1]

Additionally, it may be too simplistic to only consider asset specificity as the single factor affecting the nature of jobs under particular strategies. Transaction cost theory offers us several additional factors that will cause jobs to vary in their "temporary-appropriateness." A discussion of job attributes borrowed from transaction cost theory will be presented to examine variations among jobs within the firm as to their temporary or permanent appropriateness.

JOB ATTRIBUTES AFFECTING TRANSACTION COST LEVELS

HRM may be considered strategic to the extent that HR policies and programs minimize transaction costs (Ulrich, Yeung and Brockbank, 1992). Transaction cost theory seeks to explain organization structure in economic terms, taking into account the human aspect of individual players within the firm and the market. SHRM theoretical development using transaction cost theory (Williamson, 1975) has contemplated the use of HR activities to monitor firm employees who may otherwise shirk, free ride, or generally pursue their own goals rather than those of the firm (Jones and Wright, 1992; Ulrich et al., 1992; Wright and McMahan, 1992). HR processes such as performance appraisal and compensation are purported to be effective in encouraging employees to act in the best interest of the firm, especially when these employees have ambiguous tasks that are not easily monitorable.

The monitoring of employees gives rise to transaction costs. Employers seek the most efficient contract, that which minimizes the costs of employee monitoring while maximizing employee effort toward firm goals. A firm that is faced with filling a job that has ambiguous performance standards, for example, would be acting strategically by including the job within organizational boundaries (i.e., a permanent hire) in order to better control employee actions. In contrast, a job with definable output can be contracted for readily in the marketplace, as monitoring is easier and thus not as costly.

With its simplifying assumptions, transaction cost theory may provide

---

[1] Of course, this assumes that organizations carry out their own marketing activities. In some instances, organizations may utilize distributors to market their products for them. In other cases, the marketing function may be outsourced to specialized marketing firms.

insights into reasons underlying the decision to use temporary employees in particular job categories. Specific job attributes are purported to affect transaction cost levels and subsequent employment arrangements. Transaction cost theory may predict strategic conditions under which temporary employment may be an appropriate staffing alternative, given the objective of minimizing transaction costs. Job attributes include the transaction characteristics of asset specificity, uncertainty, and frequency of transaction occurrence, as well as task characteristics of performance ambiguity and interdependence.

Transaction characteristics

Asset specificity, as previously discussed, refers to the degree to which a particular task, process or piece of knowledge is unique to a firm (Williamson, 1979, 1985). Williamson identifies numerous types of asset specificity, of which human asset specificity is the relevant dimension for this study (Williamson, 1985). It arises because individuals acquire skills specific to an organization just by working for it (Lohtia, Brooks and Krapfel, 1994). That is, an employee may be required to develop firm-specific knowledge or skills that are not transferrable to other organizations, or he/she may be required to develop particular working relationships with other employees or with clients for the benefit of the employing organization (Lohtia et al., 1994).

To reiterate, the employee that is not permanently part of a firm hierarchy may be less willing to acquire firm-specific skills or knowledge because he/she cannot utilize such knowledge or skills in another employment setting, thus increasing his or her employment risk (Eisenhardt, 1989). The employee may not have the time to learn if the employment relationship is short-lived. He or she may also not have the opportunity to learn if the employing organization does not offer training. The training of temporaries in firm-specific skills may be a waste of resources, as the firm will not likely recoup training expenses through employee productivity due to the short-term employment arrangement (Autor, 2000; Becker, 1962). It may also be concerned with keeping firm-specific knowledge secret in order to avoid losing clients or company secrets to "non-members" of the firm (i.e., temporary employees).

In any of these situations, the firm may need to hire the employee on a permanent basis in exchange for the employee making firm-specific investments by becoming competent at firm-specific processes. On the other hand, more generalized skills and knowledge that can be transferred across different organizational settings may be adequately contracted for by the use of temporary employment (Abraham, 1988; Mangum et al., 1985; Pearce, 1993). Examples of jobs that require firm-specific expertise include managerial, administrative, or sales positions (Abraham, 1988), which are likely better carried out by permanent employees. Many clerical, professional, technical, production and service positions, on the other hand, can be conducted by temporary workers (Abraham, 1988). In general, we would expect an organization to utilize more temporary employees in positions that require little firm-specific ability (Autor, 2000).

Uncertainty is caused by complexity and change in an organization's relevant environment. Humans are boundedly rational, that is, they do not have the mental capacity to comprehend all environmental contingencies *ex ante*, which is the basis for uncertainty regarding future events (Williamson, 1981; Eisenhardt, 1989). In times of environmental turbulence (for example, rapidly changing technology), the firm's decision-makers will adjust organizational structure to reduce uncertainty. An organization is more likely to have a specific function internalized if that function deals with reduction of uncertainty. For instance, a marketing expert that is able to anticipate changing consumer tastes would be considered an important link to uncertainty reduction and would thus be hired into a permanent marketing position within the hierarchy. We would expect firms to utilize temporary employees more in job situations that deal with low levels of uncertainty.

The third transaction characteristic to be considered is *frequency of transaction occurrence*. This refers to the degree that a task recurs in an organizational process (Williamson, 1979). All else equal, a task that must be undertaken more often, human or otherwise, is more critical to the firm's functioning. This criticality increases as the importance of the task increases, especially if the task is relatively complicated or requires firm-specific abilities on the part of employees. It may become more and more expensive to contract in the market as the necessity for frequency of these contracts increases.

An example would be that of an internal corporate auditor. This auditor may work for a large holding company with many sub-units, in which auditing activities are conducted year-round because of the complexity of the corporation's operations. It would become prohibitively expensive to contract with that auditor each time a task needs to be conducted. Instead, a permanent employee would be hired to conduct such tasks on an ongoing basis, eliminating the need to negotiate numerous contracts. However, if the firm in question is a small family operation, formal audits may only need to be conducted annually. In this case, the organization would not keep an internal auditor on staff. It would contract an outside entity to conduct audits once a year. A transaction that is undertaken infrequently is better suited to temporary employment.

Task characteristics

In addition to the transaction characteristics of asset specificity, uncertainty, and frequency of transaction occurrence, two particular task attributes can affect transaction cost levels. If performance is ambiguous and/or inter-dependencies exist in the firm's technology, it is more difficult to monitor an employee's performance. Therefore, the employee would be hired into the firm in order to decrease monitoring costs and minimize the effects of opportunism.

Performance ambiguity refers to the degree of monitorability of output (Jones, 1984; Williamson, 1985; Eisenhardt, 1989). Some tasks are more easily monitorable because they have observable output, such as physical units or dollar sales. More ambiguous tasks that involve mental activities and judgments are less easily monitorable. These ambiguous tasks are not easily contracted for in the marketplace because discrete outputs cannot be readily defined. Therefore, transaction costs may be minimized by hiring permanent employees in cases where tasks are so ambiguous that specific output requirements cannot be defined and thus monitoring is difficult. For example, jobs that require managerial expertise or development of cus-tomer relationships involve tasks with ambiguous performance standards. Temporary workers may not have the motivation or opportunity to devel-op good relationships with subordinates or with firm customers since they are only going to be employed with the organization for a short time.

Implementation of specialized strategies such as differentiation, as dis-cussed earlier in this chapter, has been shown to require certain jobs with increased autonomy, and thus increased ambiguity in assessing perform-ance (Snell and Dean, 1992; Arthur, 1992). Because performance is not eas-ily monitorable, opportunism by employees can occur. Permanent employ-ment can theoretically lessen the costs of opportunism as monitoring capa-bilities increase and employees feel a sense of reciprocal responsibility with the organization.

Interdependencies among organizational members can also cause employees to become dependent upon one another's outputs. This can be conceptualized in terms of interdepartmental interdependencies in the pro-duction process as well as in terms of the team production process within departments. When employees are interdependent, they cannot function without one another. The hierarchy serves as a control mechanism, in that a group of interacting employees has monitoring capabilities over one another that are superior to that of management (Williamson, 1985). Employees may encourage each other through norms, for example, to work toward organizational goals rather than individual ones.

Alchian and Demsetz (1972) see the firm itself as a response to the prob-lems associated with the team production process. In particular, the con-tractual arrangement of the firm is caused by information costs. The firm arises because it is a less costly way of monitoring, i.e., of gathering infor-mation about the marginal productivity of interdependent organizational members (Alchian and Demsetz, 1972). Jones (1984) highlights task visi-bility in team output settings. In team production, it often becomes next to impossible to identify individuals' discrete contributions to the process. Free-riding and shirking can occur as monitoring of employees becomes more costly and individual contributions cannot be ascertained. It may become more appropriate then to internalize employees when team production is involved in order to improve monitorability as well as commitment.

Team members monitor one another in order to discourage free-riding because such self-serving behavior can affect the performance of the entire group. Even if monitoring is difficult due to complexity or ambiguity, peers have greater opportunity than management to observe and thus regulate one another's actions. Permanent hires may be encouraged to work in the firm's best interest because they feel more reciprocal obligation, while temporary employees often do not feel this sense of obligation to the firm. Furthermore, since task visibility is low in team production settings, it is difficult to determine which employees are the low performers. Managers run the risk of not knowing if temporary hires are shirking, which defeats the purpose of using temporaries in order to gain employment flexibility and resulting labor cost savings. It is more likely that permanent employment will discourage employees from shirking. Therefore, jobs having high interdependence with other jobs within a firm will be filled by permanent employees more often than by temporary employees.

THE TEMPORARY-APPROPRIATENESS OF JOBS

From the preceding discussion, we can summarize our inferences about the job attributes that may make a position more or less temporary-appropriate. We must first consider the transaction characteristics of asset specificity, uncertainty, and frequency of transaction occurrence. A job with a high degree of required firm-specific knowledge or skills is better suited to a permanent arrangement. The firm is able to secure the needed knowledge or skills for an indefinite period of time, and the employee is rewarded with long-term employment in exchange for the firm-specific knowledge or skills. A job that deals with the reduction of environmental uncertainty will be important to the firm, and permanent employees will likely be the chosen course. When transaction frequency is high, transaction costs become exorbitant as an organization must continually renegotiate employment contracts. Instead, a permanent worker is more appropriate because he or she is available to conduct the activities as needed, and the organization saves on costs of negotiating the transaction each time.

We must also consider the two particular task attributes—performance ambiguity and interdependence with other positions. As discussed in the previous section, it is difficult to negotiate employment contracts when performance standards are not easily measured. In place of costly monitoring, an organization may benefit by hiring a permanent employee to conduct tasks with ambiguous performance requirements. The reciprocal type of contract between a permanent employee and an organization will likely result in a greater feeling of mutual obligation, under which the employee may work harder on ambiguous tasks rather than shirking. Monitoring of permanent employees may also be less costly.

The interdependence of tasks within an organization means that employees must depend on one another in order to get the work done. Permanent employees will more likely be inclined to carry out their duties due to a sense of shared responsibility with employees with which their duties are interdependent. Employees also monitor one another's productivity in group settings, and a permanent employee will be more susceptible to group norms and pressures than would a temporary employee that only plans to be with a company for a short time.

In sum, types of particular jobs within a given firm will have varying degrees of asset specificity, uncertainty, frequency of transaction occurrence, performance ambiguity, and interdependence. Under transaction cost assumptions, we can predict that high degrees of the above characteristics may make a permanent arrangement the better choice of employment contract. Conversely, low degrees of these attributes may justify the use of temporary employment because the employment contract can be specified more precisely.

These job attributes are well understood in organizational literature. However, we need to gain greater insight into what causes attribute levels to vary. It is purported here that strategy will affect job attribute levels and thus will play a role in the temporary-appropriateness of jobs at the job category level. Using Porter's strategic types, we can make predictions about the levels of the five job attributes in specific job categories contingent on competitive strategy.

An organization may be divided into nine basic job categories: managerial, professional, technical, sales, clerical, craft worker, operative, laborer and service (U.S. EEOC, 1994). The content of jobs within each category may be contingent on a firm's competitive strategy. Strategy may influence the levels of asset specificity, uncertainty, frequency of transaction occurrence, performance ambiguity, and interdependence contained in the job categories.

Some of these job categories are more homogeneous than others in terms of the jobs contained within them. For instance, the operative category is made up almost entirely of jobs that deal directly with production. For other job categories, such as professional, numerous job titles may be included, making it more difficult to predict how jobs within the category will be affected by strategy. Referring to table 1, I have identified those categories expected to exhibit strong relationships to either production or marketing strategy, based on their inclusion of relatively homogeneous jobs that deal almost entirely with either the production or marketing strategy facet.

Table 1. Job Categories Affected by Strategy

Production Strategy	Marketing Strategy	Indeterminate
Technical	Sales	Managerial
Craft Workers	Service	Professional
Operatives		Clerical
Laborers		

Managerial, professional and clerical categories were assumed not to deal exclusively with either production or marketing strategy, but probably include jobs with content that deal with both strategy facets. Therefore, these job categories will likely not exhibit strong ties to either category of competitive strategy. The remaining six categories, however, are proposed to have stronger links to either production or marketing strategy. The technical, craft worker, operative and laborer categories will likely have a greater association with production strategy, while the sales and service categories will likely have a greater relation to marketing strategy.

Discussing production strategy jobs first, the choice of using either cost leadership or differentiation will likely affect the transaction cost job attributes of asset specificity, frequency of transaction occurrence, uncertainty, performance ambiguity and interdependence in production-related jobs within the technical, craft worker, operative, and laborer job categories. Jobs that are integrally involved with the product transformation process will be more affected than will jobs that deal with other aspects of the organization.

Taking one example, jobs in the technical category will differ in their levels of job attributes according to firm strategy. It is predicted that technical jobs (i.e., technicians, drafters, computer programmers) in differentiating firms will have higher levels of asset specificity, uncertainty, frequency of transaction occurrence and interdependencies than will technical jobs in cost leadership firms. Technical jobs are highly related to the production process, which will differ according to the type of competitive product strategy chosen. Therefore, it is predicted that differentiators, regardless of market focus, will choose to utilize more permanent employees than will cost leadership firms in technical positions.

Craft workers, operatives, and laborers, being closely tied to the production process, will also be less temporary appropriate under the differentiation strategy than under the cost leader strategy. These production workers will require higher levels of asset specificity and will also likely be organized into team production settings. Market focus will not likely be a major influence on job attributes of craft, operative or laborer positions.

Choice of marketing strategy, either breadth or focus, will affect jobs that deal with the process of marketing an organization's product or service. Job attributes of marketing-related positions (i.e., sales and service categories) will be impacted in that as firms become more focused on particular market segments, marketing jobs will become more important to the organization for survival and profitability.

Sales and service jobs will be more suitable to permanent employment under the focus marketing strategy than under the breadth strategy (for both differentiators and cost leaders). Sales and service staff will require higher levels of firm-specific assets, will deal with uncertainty in customer markets, and will work interdependently with other organizational functions in the marketing effort. This effort will be on-going, which increases transaction frequency, and will be ambiguous in terms of performance standards.

STRATEGIC TEMPORARY STAFFING

The purpose of this study is to examine temporary employment from a strategic perspective. An organization's competitive strategy is predicted to impact the effectiveness of using temporary workers. Transaction cost theory (Williamson, 1985) combined with Porter's competitive framework (1980) may provide insights into the determinants behind the decision to use temporary employees in organizations. This may aid our understanding of organizational and job attributes that may impact the effectiveness of including temporary employees in firm staffing strategy. Strategic use of temporaries is purported to be a function of a firm's need for firm-specific activities. The effect of strategy on transaction characteristics including asset specificity, uncertainty, frequency of transaction occurrence, performance ambiguity and interdependencies may predict the effectiveness of using temporaries within particular job categories.

The benefit of flexibility is a chief reason given by organizations for using contingent employment (Abraham, 1988; Cooper, 1995; Mangum et al., 1985; SHRM, 1998). Employers can easily adjust employment levels in response to demand fluctuations by using temporaries only when needed. However, an organization's decision to use temporary workers may in fact backfire if the firm's strategy is ignored. The fact that temporaries add flexibility to employee levels is an established point. A problem is that using them may result in an erosion of competitive advantage due to lack of loyalty, of established contacts and stable customer relations, or of firm-specific abilities (Cooper, 1995). For firms that follow a cost leadership strategy (Porter, 1980) the benefits of temporary employment usage may not erode competitive advantage. These firms typically use mass production as a means of increasing market share and thus gain competitive advantage in this way. A majority of jobs are typically low-skill with low wages. Employees are for the most part interchangeable. Temporaries might be quite appropriate in a cost leadership setting.

Those firms pursuing differentiation as a strategy (Porter, 1980), however, may find that temporary employees do not help them gain competitive advantage. Differentiation involves developing unique products and/or services, and consumers expect to pay more for them. Use of temporaries may damage these firms' ability to differentiate themselves through superior production or service processes. Temporary employees may not feel as strong a commitment to the organization as permanent employees. Temporaries may not have the necessary skills in order to make the differentiation strategy work. The inappropriateness of temporary worker usage may be to the detriment of firm performance. This interactional effect of temporary employment and organization strategy on subsequent organizational performance is the focus of this book.

The connection of competitive strategy and temporary employment is thus important to examine. Differentiating firms should utilize a greater number of permanent rather than temporary employees, which should benefit overall performance. Cost leader firms will likely utilize a greater number of temporary employees to their benefit. Similarly, firms with a focus marketing strategy should use a greater number of permanent employees, while firms following a breadth marketing strategy should utilize a greater number of temporary employees.

The use of appropriate levels of temporary employment according to a firm's competitive strategy is predicted to have positive effects on firm performance. The agreement or "fit" (Venkatraman, 1989; Youndt et al., 1995) between overall temporary employment usage and competitive strategy should positively impact firm performance. A lack of fit, implying inappropriate use of temporaries under a particular strategy, should negatively impact firm performance.

The underlying reason that performance will be impacted by the fit between temporary staffing and strategy is that transaction costs are affected. A high use of temporary employees when more specialization is needed to implement strategy (i.e., under differentiation or focus) may result in employment contracts being misspecified and subsequently not fully carried out by temporaries. This will result in higher future transaction costs to remedy inappropriate contracting. If, on the other hand, an organization does not take full advantage of using temporaries when it may be cost-effective to do so (i.e., under cost leadership or breadth), the organization may be expending too much on transaction costs associated with the permanent employment arrangement when in reality permanence is not needed. The next chapter introduces specific hypotheses regarding the strategic effectiveness of temporary employees.

CHAPTER FOUR

Hypothesis Development

A STRATEGIC MODEL OF TEMPORARY STAFFING

From the preceding discussion, it is clear that the temporary staffing phe-nomenon needs to be explored much further. Not only is empirical research into its benefits and costs limited (Davis-Blake and Uzzi, 1993; Herer and Harel, 1998; Nollen and Axel, 1996; Pfeffer and Baron, 1988), firm con-tingencies (e.g., strategy) and job attributes have also virtually been ignored. Therefore, I have developed in this book a strategic model of tem-porary staffing. The resulting model integrates overall as well as job cate-gory temporary employee usage, organizational strategy, and subsequent

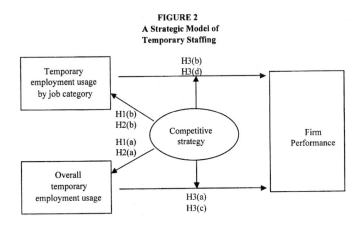

FIGURE 2
A Strategic Model of
Temporary Staffing

effects on organizational performance. The research model is presented in figure 2.

Using transaction cost assumptions, we can make predictions about an organization's use of temporary employees under particular strategic contingencies. First, choice of strategy will affect the overall nature of jobs within the organization, based on the extent of asset specificity required of employees. This in turn will affect the organization's overall use of temporaries.

Second, recognizing that jobs within each firm will be diverse, we can then predict the particular job categories more likely to be affected by strategic choice. These job categories will be affected in the amount of temporary employment used within, more so than job categories less related to strategic imperatives.

Last, agreement or fit of business strategy and temporary employment usage is hypothesized to positively impact firm performance. Temporary employment usage is more consistent with the cost leadership and breadth strategies, so we expect to find a positive relationship between temporary employment and firm performance under these strategies. Temporary employment is much less appropriately utilized in differentiation and focus settings. Therefore, we expect to find that a negative relationship exists between temporary employment and firm performance under these two strategies.

Referring to figure 2, the strategic model of temporary staffing examines temporary employment usage as a part of an organization's staffing strategy. I hypothesize that an organization's competitive strategy will influence its choice to use temporary employees more or less extensively. Production strategy and marketing strategy are considered separately, with effects at the organization and job category levels. Then, the moderating effect of strategy between temporary employment and organizational performance will be hypothesized.

PRODUCTION STRATEGY AND TEMPORARY EMPLOYMENT

Overall, firms that utilize a cost leadership production strategy should more likely utilize temporary employees than firms following a differentiation strategy. This logic follows from the discussion in previous chapters regarding asset specificity. Some types of tasks are more suited to temporary or to permanent employment. Differentiating firms will require employees with a wide variety of skills and training such that they can perform a diversity of tasks (Arthur, 1992; Snell and Dean, 1991). These employees will necessarily have some discretion over activities because the work is less standardized and will tend to be more organization-specific in nature (Arthur, 1992; Porter, 1980). These types of activities are better suited to the permanent employment arrangement. Conversely, cost leaders utilize more standardized production activities and will thus have more control over employee activities. In this case, temporary employees with generalized skills may serve as a more cost-effective resource. Extent of overall temporary employee usage should differ between these two types of competitive strategies.

Hypothesis one (a): Organizations with a cost leadership production strategy will overall utilize temporary employees to a greater extent than will organizations with a differentiation production strategy.

It may be that, rather than impacting the entire organization's jobs, choice of production strategy may only significantly affect those jobs integrally involved in the production process. That is, we may only find that some jobs are affected by production strategy while others are little affected. The degree of a job category's transaction attributes (i.e., asset specificity, uncertainty, frequency of transaction occurrence, performance ambiguity and interdependence) should be highly impacted by an organization's choice to be either a cost leader or differentiator. Cost leader firms should find that lower levels of these attributes exist in production-related positions, while differentiators should see much higher attribute levels.

The job categories most likely to be affected by production strategy include the technical, craft worker, operative and laborer categories. These categories contain higher percentages of jobs that deal with the firm's product transformation process. We expect to find that extent of temporary employment usage will differ according to production strategy in these job categories, with cost leaders reflecting a higher use of temporaries than that of differentiators.

Hypothesis one (b): Organizations with a cost leadership production strategy will utilize temporary employees to a greater extent in the technical, craft worker, operative and laborer categories than will organizations with a differentiation production strategy.

MARKETING STRATEGY AND TEMPORARY EMPLOYMENT

Additionally, marketing strategy will affect temporary employee utilization. Organizations that decide to concentrate on narrow market segments (i.e., focus strategy) will require a higher degree of firm-specific activities than those who cater to a larger breadth market. Conversely, organizations that choose to market their products widely may find that temporary employees are more useful in carrying out marketing activities as asset specificity requirements are lessened. Marketing strategy is thus hypothesized to also affect the extent of overall temporary employment usage.

Hypothesis two (a): Organizations with a breadth marketing strategy will overall utilize temporary employees to a greater extent than will organizations with a focus marketing strategy.

It is expected that effect of marketing strategy will be more pronounced on those jobs that directly deal with the organization's marketing efforts. Jobs' transaction attributes of asset specificity, uncertainty, transaction frequency, performance ambiguity and interdependence will rise as a firm moves its marketing strategy toward a more focused audience. Breadth marketers, in contrast, will find lower levels of these attributes as they use more broad-based marketing techniques.

Breadth marketers should be able to more effectively utilize temporary workers, as many of the marketing tasks will be simpler and more structured. Conversely, organizations with a focus strategy may find that the transaction costs associated with their marketing positions demand more permanent employment arrangements. The job categories most closely tied to the marketing function are sales and service. I expect that levels of temporary employment will vary within these two job categories based on an organization's marketing strategy.

> **Hypothesis two (b): Organizations with a breadth marketing strategy will utilize temporary employees to a greater extent in the sales and service job categories than will organizations with a focus marketing strategy.**

ORGANIZATIONAL PERFORMANCE

The next relationship to be examined in figure 2 relates to the association between the extent of temporary employment usage and organizational performance. One factor that may affect organization performance levels is the "match" or "mismatch" between strategy and temporary employee usage (Venkatraman, 1989; Youndt et al., 1995). Fit can be conceptualized in numerous ways. One way of examining the fit between variables is through moderation (Venkatraman, 1989). That is, variables "agree" or "fit" if support can be found for specified moderating effects. It is thus defined here as the moderating effect of strategy on the relationship between temporary employee usage and organizational performance.

We expect to find a positive effect of the use of temporary employment under a cost leadership strategy on organizational performance. Overall, temporary employee usage is more appropriate in the cost leadership setting than in the differentiation setting because of the organizational processes that are undertaken. We also expect to find a negative interaction between the use of temporaries and a differentiation strategy in influencing organizational performance. A mismatch occurs when temporaries are used too heavily in a differentiation setting or too little in a cost leadership setting, which may negatively impact organizational performance.

Hypothesis three (a): Production strategy moderates the relationship between overall temporary employment usage and organizational performance such that overall temporary employment usage will be positively related to performance under a cost leadership strategy but negatively related under a differentiation strategy.

A stronger effect may be found when only production-related job category temporary levels are examined, rather than overall temporary usage. We expect the same moderating relationship of production strategy to exist at the job category level for cost leader and differentiator organizations' performance levels.

Hypothesis three (b): Production strategy moderates the relationship between temporary employment usage in the technical, craft worker, operative and laborer job categories and organizational performance such that temporary usage in these job categories will be positively related to performance under a cost leadership strategy but negatively related under a differentiation strategy.

Similarly, extent of market focus will also affect the fit between strategy and temporary employment usage. Firms with a wider (e.g., breadth) marketing strategy will likely provide a more appropriate setting for temporaries than will focus firms. Overall, organizations in a breadth marketing scenario will likely enjoy performance benefits from using temporary employees because jobs will be better suited to the temporary arrangement. Conversely, firms utilizing a focus marketing strategy will benefit more overall from the permanent employment arrangement.

Hypothesis three (c): Marketing strategy moderates the relationship between overall temporary employment usage and organizational performance such that overall temporary employment usage will be positively related to performance under a breadth strategy but negatively related under a focus strategy.

The moderating effect of marketing strategy on the relationship between temporary usage and performance may be more significant in particular job categories relating to the marketing function, namely the sales and service job categories. Temporary employment usage within these two job categories may have important performance implications. The positive relationship between temporary usage and breadth strategy, as well as the negative association between temporary usage and focus strategy in the sales and service areas should result in higher organizational performance.

Hypothesis three (d): Marketing strategy moderates the relationship between temporary employment usage in the sales and service job categories and organizational performance such that temporary usage in these job categories will be positively related to performance under a breadth strategy but negatively related under a focus strategy.

CHAPTER FIVE

Methods

SAMPLE AND SURVEY

The study's target sample consisted of 735 organizations included in the Hoover's Handbook of American Business (1996). The Hoover's Handbook is published annually. Public as well as private organizations are chosen for inclusion in the Handbook for being the largest and most influential companies in America. Four general criteria for selecting these organizations include size, growth, visibility and breadth of coverage across industries (Hoover's Handbook, 1996). The Handbook includes company profiles as well as selected information on company officers and key financial data.

Before discussing the methods and variables, background information is needed regarding the data utilized in this study. It is important to recognize the shortcomings of existing data regarding the contingent employment phenomenon. Data in past research has typically been acquired from national governmental entities. These data, by their very nature, do not include information at the organization level. Aggregate census data regarding contingent employment usage are available at the national level from the Bureau of Labor Statistics, and this information is broken down into types of jobs or contingent employment arrangements (e.g., contract, temporary, leased employees, etc.).

However, these data cannot be connected to specific organizations' use of temporary employment included in such samples, which eliminates the ability to assess firm-level variables such as organizational strategy, types of jobs filled by contingent workers, and effects on organizational performance. Therefore, an aim of this study was to obtain such organization-level data. A limitation of the sample was that the extent to which respondent firms use temporary employment was not known. The Hoover's Handbook includes a random configuration of firms that will likely have differing levels of temporary employee use. All responding firms used temporary employment in their human resource strategy. However, it was not known whether companies exist within the larger database that do not utilize temporary employees.

A pretest of the survey instrument was conducted. Nineteen human resource executives who were members of an advisory board to the Center for Human Resource Management at Texas A&M University were asked to pretest the survey. Ten of these executives responded, for a response rate of 52.6%. The survey was revised as suggested by these professionals before being sent to the organizations in the sample. The human resource executives' organizations all reported using temporary employees. They provided useful feedback regarding the survey's clarity and format. Additionally, these executives offered insights into the manner in which firms may keep records of their temporary employee usage (i.e., by job category, functional department, or both).

Target respondents to the subsequent research survey were the top human resource managers of organizations in the Hoover's Handbook. An additional survey was included to be distributed to a top operations manager of each organization. A cover letter was included with the survey in order to explain the study's goals. Organizations were offered a summary of results in exchange for their participation. The survey instrument is included in appendix A.

Approximately six weeks after the initial mailout, three research assistants were hired to make follow-up phone calls to approximately three-quarters of the non-responding organizations. The purpose of the study was again explained and a summary of results offered in exchange for participation. Organizational representatives were then asked for a verbal commitment to fill out the survey instrument. Those representatives who agreed to participate were either faxed or mailed a copy of the survey for themselves and also a copy for a second organizational representative to fill out. After a second six week period, another round of follow-up phone calls was conducted by the author and one of the research assistants previously utilized.

VARIABLES

Data on the following variables were gathered through the survey and from the CompuStat database. Individual variables were examined and tested for normality using the Wald statistic (Greene, 1993). Some researchers argue that normality is not as critical for researchers in the social sciences, as long as care is taken in sampling, analysis, and interpretation of parametric statistical results (Kerlinger, 1986). However, I attempted to normalize variable distributions as much as possible in order to improve statistical accuracy. Variables with non-normal distributions were transformed as noted.

Dependent variables

Overall extent of temporary employee usage (OVERTEMP). Respondents were asked to indicate the approximate percentage of total labor hours worked by temporaries for their last fiscal reporting year. (See appendix A, part III, number 1). The percentage of overall temporary employee usage was non-normally distributed. A logarithmic transformation was used, which normalized the data distribution.

Job category temporary employee usage (PRODTEMP, MKTTEMP). Survey items were also included that assessed temporary employment usage by job category (managerial, professional, technical, sales, clerical, craft, operative, laborer, and service). Job categories that were thought to be generally more related to either production or marketing strategy were identified and their percentages combined additively into categories representing production-related and marketing-related temporary usage respectively. The production-related index (PRODTEMP) was comprised of the sum of the technical, craft worker, operative and laborer category percentages. The marketing-related index (MKTTEMP) was comprised of the sum of the sales and service category percentages. (See appendix A, part III).

The production-related job category index was normally distributed. The marketing-related job category index was not normally distributed. However, transformation of this variable provided some difficulties. Due to a large number of zero values, the use of a logarithmic transformation was not possible, as the log of zero is indeterminate. The square root of the index improved the distribution, but normality was still not achieved. However, this transformation provided the best option so it was utilized. The variable MKTTEMP is, therefore, the square root of the original marketing-related temporary employment percentage.

Organizational performance (PERF, ROI). Firms were asked in the survey to provide perceptual measures of organizational performance (see appendix A, part V). It was expected that human resource representatives may or may not have familiarity with actual firm performance numbers. Perceptual measures of performance have been used before in surveys of human resource managers (Delaney and Huselid, 1996) and of managers in general (Beard and Dess, 1981; Youndt et al., 1996). These measures appear to serve as relatively accurate representations of firm performance (Venkatraman and Ramanujam, 1986). Respondents were asked to rate their organizations on a percentage scale from bottom 10% to top 10% in ten-percent intervals. They were asked to compare their organizations to their competitors on operating efficiency, quality, service, sales, profitability, and market share. An overall performance index (PERF) was developed by averaging these six percentages. Coefficient alpha for this index was 0.91 (Cronbach, 1951).

Performance data (ROI, ROA) was also obtained through the CompuStat database for publicly held firms within the sample. Both the ROI (return on investment) and ROA (return on assets) variables failed to pass the Wald normality test. In both variables outlying data points caused this to occur. One company had a significantly higher ROA value than the others, and the ROI variable contained one low and one high outlier. When these outliers were omitted, both ROA and ROI passed the normality test. However, since these outlying numbers were true numbers and not errors, some may argue that they should be included in the analysis (McClave and Benson, 1988). I chose to use the full ROI and ROA values rather than omitting the outliers for this reason.

ROI and ROA were compared with perceptual data from the survey to assess consistency. The performance index from the survey did not have significant correlations with ROA or ROI. This is likely due to the inclusion of more subjective performance indicators such as quality and service in the survey performance index, while the objective ROA and ROI are purely accounting-related figures. ROA and ROI were, as expected, highly significantly correlated with one another. ROI has been used more frequently than ROA in business strategy research (Jacobson, 1987; Venkatraman and Ramanujam, 1986) and is thought to be more representative of firm performance than ROA (Shapiro, 1989). Therefore, I chose to run subsequent regression analyses using the subjective performance index (PERF) and the objective ROI performance numbers to more fully test hypotheses three (a) through three (d), that strategy moderates the temporary usage—performance relationship.

Independent variables

Strategy (PRODSTRAT, MKTSTRAT). Competitive strategy was measured through several items on the firm survey (see appendix A, part VI). The items asked respondents to rate their organizations as significantly lower or higher than their perceived industry competitors on product price and specialization as well as on market focus. The survey included seven items using a 7-point Likert-scale. Three were cost leader-differentiator items, numbers 1, 2, and 7. Four were focus-breadth items, numbers 3, 4, 8 (reverse coded) and 9 (reverse coded). Two cost leader-differentiator items used a zero to 100% scale, numbers 5 and 6 (reverse coded). These two percentage scale items were converted to the 7-point Likert scale as well, by dividing the percentages by 14.29 (100 divided by 7).

All items were initially combined into two overall indices based on *a priori* assumptions of their relatedness to either the cost leader-differentiator dimension or the focus-breadth dimension. This was to provide a continuous measure of production strategy and market strategy. Values of the production strategy responses (five items) were averaged, as were the market strategy responses (four items). Higher values represent lesser amounts of required asset specificity (i.e., cost leader and breadth). Lower values represent higher degrees of required asset specificity (i.e., differentiator and focus). In both cases, the strategy index values are theorized to be positively related to the use of temporary employment (i.e., a higher production strategy value, representing lower asset specificity, should be associated with a higher use of temporary employment).

Coefficient alphas (Cronbach, 1951) for the original production and market strategy indices were poor (.62 and .40 respectively). Therefore, I conducted a factor analysis to assess the actual number of factors in the underlying data. Four factors emerged, revealing possible problems with item wording. I reduced the number of items to three for the production strategy (items 5, 6 and 7) and to two for the marketing strategy (items 8 and 9), which improved alpha estimates to .71 and .70 respectively (Cronbach, 1951). These reduced indices were used in subsequent analyses.

Control variables

Several variables were operationalized in order to control for differences among sample firms. As the sample size in this study was small, I included in the regression analyses only those control variables that turned out to be significant in order to preserve power.

Organization size (SIZE). Organizational size was operationalized by number of permanent employees as identified on the survey (see Appendix A, part I). Number of employees was also obtained from the CompuStat database (SIZECOMP), as was total asset value (ASSETS) which is another proxy for organization size. As in previous research, all of these data were non-normally distributed. The three variables were subsequently logarithmically transformed and passed the Wald test for normality. SIZE, the log of number of employees from the survey, was significantly correlated with SIZECOMP (log of employees from CompuStat) and marginally significantly related to ASSETS (log of assets from CompuStat). Therefore, I felt it appropriate to use the survey information, as it was apparently related to the archival data. Additionally, the survey data included both public and non-public organizations while the CompuStat data did not.

Industry (INMFG, INSVC, INDOTHER). Sample firm industry membership was assessed through the survey and through the Hoover's Handbook. Each firm was asked to provide the industry from which it obtained a majority of its sales. Industry membership was included as it may differentially influence the use of temporary employees as well as performance. Cross-checked for accuracy with the survey and based on information from the Hoover's Handbook, organizations were classified into one of three general industry categories: manufacturing, service or other. These categories were dummy-coded, with the other category serving as the referent.

Unionization. Survey respondents were asked to provide their percentage of unionized permanent workers. Data showed that 31 of the 38 responding companies had unionization percentages of 2% or less. The data's distribution was extremely non-normal, and attempts to normalize the data were not successful. As most organizations had little or no union representation, this variable was dropped from further analysis.

Location. The area in which an organization is located may affect temporary staffing levels. Factors such as level of unemployment, number of temporary agencies, or availability of labor with particular skills may impact the choice whether to use temporary employees. Sample firms were grouped into five geographic areas in order to eliminate possible location effects. These areas of the U.S. were labeled as middle states, northeast, south, west, and southwest. This variable was dummy-coded, with southwest serving as the referent category.

CHAPTER SIX

Results

A total of 136 organizations (18.5%) responded to the survey request. Of these, 93 companies declined to participate in the study. Reasons for non-participation included corporate policy, lack of time or manpower, and, perhaps most importantly, lack of centralized information regarding use of temporary employment. An additional 64 organizations (8.7%) were sent one, and in some cases two, follow-up surveys after securing their verbal agreement by phone to participate. These surveys were not returned. The reasons for non-participation by these organizations is unknown.

A total of 43 companies (5.9%) returned at least one survey. Of these, 38 returned at least one useable response. (One organization returned two useable responses, but one was dropped from further analysis to preserve consistency.) Therefore, the final number of organizations included in the analysis was 38, reflecting a useable response rate to the survey of 5.2%. Of these, 30 of the 38 organizations were publicly traded firms.

These organizations were located in twenty-four different states. One state contained six organizations, two states had four organizations, three states contained two organizations, and eighteen states had one organization each. When classified into location, nine were located in the middle states, six were located in the northeast, six were located in the southwest, nine were located in the south, and eight were located in the west. All responding organizations cited the use of temporary employment to some extent.[1]

A business profile of the responding organizations' major businesses is shown in table 2. As table 2 reflects, a wide array of businesses were present among the organizations. These companies were classified into one of

---

[1] In fact, only one organizational representative out of the 200 I had contact with stated that his organization did not use any temporary employees.

three industry categories. Industry membership consisted of 9 manufacturing (23.7%), 17 service (44.7%) and twelve other (31.6%; consisting of 4 natural resources, 7 trade and 1 diversified).

Table 2. Business Profile of Respondent Organizations*

Agriculture - beef and cattle (1)	Malt beverages
poultry (2)	Managed health care
Aircraft and electronics systems manufacturing	Offshore construction/power generation
Airline (2)	Petroleum refining and marketing
Apparel manufacturing and	Pharmaceuticals distribution
distribution (2)	Publishing
Computer distribution	Real estate development
Computer manufacturing – printers	Refinery equipment
Electronics - distribution	Retail stores (2)
Electronics - retail	Social expressions (greeting cards)
Engineering and construction (2)	Specialty chemicals
Financial services (3)	Utility - electric (4)
	- natural gas
Forest products	
Grocery distribution	
Insurance (2)	

*Unless otherwise noted, only one organization per category

Of the thirty-eight respondents who filled out the surveys, all but two held HR positions within their organizations. The two non-HR respondents held the titles of "systems supervisor" and "business services manager." Position titles for the thirty-six HR respondents included the terms "senior vice president" or "director" (11); "vice president" (2); "assistant vice president" (1); "manager" or "coordinator" (2); "senior representative," "senior specialist" or "supervisor" (4); "assistant" or "representative" (5); and "HR consultant" (1). Average tenure for all respondents was 4½ years, with a range from three months to twenty-four years.

An analysis of outside data was conducted when available in order to minimize common method variance (Campbell and Fiske, 1959; Podsakoff and Organ, 1986). Performance data (ROI and ROA), total number of employees, and asset values were collected for the publicly held firms as a check on information gathered from the surveys. Additionally, sending surveys to multiple respondents within organizations was planned to serve as a reliability check. However, this was not possible, as only one company out of the thirty-eight returned two useable responses. Therefore, cross-checking of survey information with archival data was the only available reliability check for this study, and furthermore this was only available for the publicly traded organizations. Means, standard deviations, and correlations for all variables are shown in table 3.

TABLE 3. Means, Standard Deviations, and Correlations

Variables	Mean	s.d.	1	2	3	4	5	6	7	8	9	10	11	12
1. SIZE	8.86	1.51												
2. SIZECOMP	9.84	1.09	.41[b]											
3. ASSETS	8.58	1.35	.31[a]	.50[c]										
4. INDMFG	0.24	0.43	.07	-.04	-.33[a]									
5. INDSVC	0.45	0.50	.21	-.01	.50[c]	-.50[c]								
6. INDOTHER	0.29	0.46	-.31[a]	.08	-.18	-.36[b]	-.57[c]							
7. PRODSTRAT	2.87	1.49	.12	.00	.07	-.11	-.03	.17						
8. MKTSTRAT	5.49	1.44	.00	.38[b]	-.25	.42[c]	-.25	-.18	-.21					
9. OVERTEMP	1.74	1.08	.02	-.25	-.20	.06	-.07	-.08	.17	.11				
10. PRODTEMP	32.35	28.19	-.33[a]	-.36[a]	-.39[a]	.22	-.40[b]	.23	.12	.13	.23			
11. MKTTEMP	1.55	2.81	.38[b]	.32	.11	-.13	-.02	.10	-.17	-.10	.13	-.29		
12. PERF	74.22	13.88	.18	.28	.00	.02	-.03	.02	-.04	.14	-.12	-.26	.09	
13. ROI	6.60	5.04	.34[a]	-.02	-.09	.09	.05	-.08	.22	-.10	.29	.45[b]	.02	.12

[a] $p < .10$
[b] $p < .05$
[c] $p < .01$

Hypotheses were tested using hierarchical regression analysis. Sets of regression equations were developed for the following dependent variables: extent of overall temporary employee usage, extent of job category temporary employee usage, and organizational performance. The incremental amount of variance explained by relevant independent variables over that explained by variables entered earlier in the regressions indicate whether the hypotheses were supported.

Preliminary regression equations were run with control variables included. Controls included organization size, industry, and location. In the regression equations at the job category level, log of employees (SIZE) was at least marginally significantly predictive, so it was retained in all equations. No other control variables were significant in the regression equations, so they were excluded from further analyses.

Equation one (a) regressed the overall index of temporary employee usage (OVERTEMP) on organization size (SIZE) in step one and on production strategy (PRODSTRAT) in step two. A significant incremental R^2 for the production strategy coefficient in step two would support hypothesis one (a), which stated that organizations will overall utilize temporary employees to a greater extent than will organizations with a differentiation strategy. Results are shown in table 4. Only 3% incremental variance in overall temporary employee usage was explained by production strategy, which was non-significant. Therefore, hypothesis one (a) was not supported.

Table 4. Hierarchical Regression Analysis, Equation One (a)

Dependent Variable: Log of temporary employee usage (OVERTEMP)

Independent variable	R^2	$R^2 change$	*p of change*
Step One: Log of Employees (SIZE)	.00	.00	.93
Step Two: Product Strategy (PRODSTRAT)	.03	.03	.35

Cumulative R^2 = 0.03; F = 0.46; p = 0.63; d.f. = 2, 30

Equation one (b) tested hypothesis one (b) regarding job-category effects of production strategy on temporary employee usage in production-related job categories. This equation regressed the production job category usage of temporary employees (PRODTEMP) on organization size (SIZE) in step one and on production strategy (PRODSTRAT) in step two. A significant incremental R^2 for the production strategy variable in step two would support hypothesis one (b), which stated that production strategy will affect job category usage of temporary employees in production-related jobs. Results are shown in table 5. No significant variance was explained by production strategy (R^2 = 0.03, n.s.). Therefore, hypothesis one (b) was not supported.

Table 5. Hierarchical Regression Analysis, Equation One (b)

Dependent Variable: Temporary employee usage by job categories relating to production strategy (PRODTEMP)

Independent variable	R^2	R^2change	p of change
Step One: Log of Employees (SIZE)	.11	.11	.06
Step Two: Product Strategy (PRODSTRAT)	.14	.03	.36

Cumulative R^2 = 0.14; F =2.286; p = 0.12; d.f. = 2, 29

In equation two (a), overall temporary employee usage (OVERTEMP) was regressed on organization size (SIZE) in step one and on marketing strategy (MKTSTRAT) in step two. A significant incremental R^2 for the marketing strategy variable in step two would support hypothesis two (a), which stated that an organization's marketing strategy affects overall temporary employee usage. Results are shown in table 6. Only 1% of incremental variance was explained, which was non-significant. Thus, hypothesis two (a) was not supported.

Table 6. Hierarchical Regression Analysis, Equation Two (a)

Dependent Variable: Log of temporary employee usage (OVERTEMP)

Independent variable	R^2	R^2change	p of change
Step One: Log of Employees (SIZE)	.00	.00	.93
Step Two: Marketing Strategy (MKTSTRAT)	.01	.01	.56

Cumulative R^2 = 0.01; F = 0.18; p = 0.84; d.f. = 2, 30

Equation two (b) tested hypothesis two (b), which stated that marketing strategy significantly predicts the percentage of temporaries used in marketing-related job categories. In this equation, marketing-related job category temporary employee usage (MKTTEMP) was regressed on organizational size (SIZE) in step one and on marketing strategy (MKT-STRAT) in step two. A significant amount of variance explained in step two would support hypothesis two (b). Results are shown in table 7. The incremental R^2 for step two was .01, which was non-significant. Therefore, hypothesis two (b) was not supported.

Table 7. Hierarchical Regression Analysis, Equation Two (b)

Dependent Variable: Temporary employee usage by job categories relating to marketing strategy (MKTTEMP)

Independent variable	R^2	R^2 change	p of change
Step One: Log of Employees (SIZE)	.14	.14	.03
Step Two: Marketing Strategy (MKTSTRAT)	.15	.01	.59

Cumulative R^2 = 0.15; F = 2.58; p = 0.09; d.f. = 2, 29

Equation three (a) regressed organizational performance (either PERF or ROI) on organization size (SIZE) in step one, on overall temporary employee usage (OVERTEMP) in step two, on production strategy (PROD-STRAT) in step three, and on the interaction between overall temporary employee usage and production strategy in step four. A significant incremental R^2 for the interaction between strategy and temporary usage in step four would support hypothesis three (a), which stated that production strategy moderates the overall temporary usage-performance relationship such that temporary employment usage and performance will be positively related for cost leader firms and will be negatively related for differentiating firms (Cohen, 1968; Stone and Hollenbeck, 1984). Results are shown in table 8.

Equation three (a) was run twice, first with the subjective performance index (PERF) as the dependent variable, and second with ROI as the dependent variable. In equation three (a) with the subjective performance index (PERF) as the dependent variable, the interaction between temporary employee usage and production strategy in step four explained significant incremental variance. An additional 31% of the variance in the subjective performance index (p = .00) was explained by this interaction.

The moderating effect of production strategy on the temporary usage-performance relationship was as hypothesized when the subjective performance index was the dependent variable. As seen in figure 3 (with organization size held constant at its mean), under a differentiation strategy there is a negative relationship between overall temporary usage and performance, while under a cost leadership strategy the relationship is positive.

Table 8. Hierarchical Regression Analysis, Equation Three (a)

Dependent Variable: Performance		PERF			ROI	
Independent variable	R^2	R^2 change	p of change	R^2	R^2 change	p of change
Step One:						
Log of Employees (SIZE)	.03	.03	.32	.11	.11	.09
Step Two:						
Log of temp. employee usage (OVERTEMP)	.05	.02	.48	.19	.08	.14
Step Three:						
Product Energy (PRODSTRAT)	.05	.00	.83	.21	.02	.48
Step Four:						
Product X temp. usage (OVERTEMP X PRODSTRAT)	.36	.31	.00	.28	.07	.17

Cumulative R^2 = 0.36
F = 3.97
p = 0.01
d.f. = 4, 28

Cumulative R^2 = 0.28
F = 2.06
p = 0.12
d.f. = 4, 21

FIGURE 3
Interaction of Production Strategy and
Overall Temporary Usage on Performance (PERF)
in Equation 3(a)

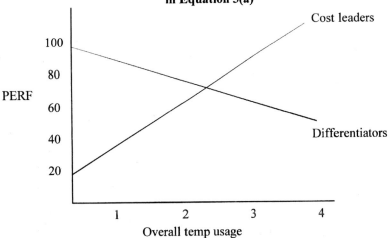

The overall regression model is highly significant (p = .01) and all beta coefficients are also highly significant (see table 9). Thus, hypothesis three (a), that production strategy moderates the overall temp usage – performance relationship such that the relationship is positive for cost leaders and negative for differentiators, received support when the subjective performance index was used as the dependent variable.

In equation three (a), when ROI was used as the dependent variable, the interaction of production strategy and temporary employee usage was nonsignificant (incremental R^2 of .07, p = .17). Results again are shown in table 8. Thus hypothesis three (a) was not supported when performance was operationalized as ROI.

Equation three (b) regressed organizational performance (PERF, ROI) on organization size (SIZE) in step one, on production-related job category temporary usage (PRODTEMP) in step two, on production strategy (PRODSTRAT) in step three, and on the interaction between PRODTEMP and PRODSTRAT in step four. A significant amount of variance explained by the interaction term in step four would support hypothesis three (b), that strategy moderates the relationship between production-related temporary employee use and organizational performance such that a positive relationship would be revealed for cost leaders and a negative relationship would be shown for differentiators (Cohen, 1964; Stone and Hollenbeck, 1984). Results are shown in table 10. With the subjective performance index (PERF) as the dependent variable, none of the variables explained significant variance. Thus, hypothesis three (b) was not supported by this equation.

Table 9. Results of Regression Equation Three (a)

Dependent Variable: Performance	PERF	ROI
	Complete model beta coefficient	*Complete model beta coefficient*
Independent variable	*(F=3.97, p=.01)*	*(F=2.06, p=.12)*
Log of Employees (SIZE)	4.24***	.63
Log of Temp. Employee usage (OVERTEMP)	−15.30***	3.57*
Product Strategy (PRODSTRAT)	−12.58***	2.55
Product X Temp. Usage (OVERTEMP X PRODSTRAT)	5.76***	−0.98
Constant	69.49***	−7.39

***p<.01; **p<.05; *p<.10

Table 10. Hierarchical Regression Analysis, Equation Three (b)

Dependent Variable: Performance		PERF			ROI	
Independent variable	R^2	R^2 change	*p of* change	R^2	R^2 change	*p of* change
Step One:						
Log of Employees (SIZE)	.03	.03	.33	.11	.11	.10
Step Two:						
Temp. employee usage by Production Job Categories (PRODTEMP)	.08	.05	.23	.47	.36	.00
Step Three:						
Product Strategy (PRODSTRAT)	.08	.00	.90	.48	.01	.61
Step Four:						
Product X temp. usage (OVERTEMP X PRODSTRAT)	.11	.03	.35	.55	.07	.08

Cumulative R^2 = 0.11	Cumulative R^2 = 0.55
F = 0.83	F = 6.19
p = 0.52	p = 0.002
d.f. = 4, 27	d.f. = 4, 20

With ROI as the dependent variable, step four reflects a marginally significant amount of incremental variance, with an R^2 of .07 (p = .08, see table 10). Results of the complete equation are shown in table 11. The complete model is highly significant (p = .002) and all beta coefficients are at least marginally significant. The interaction term has a marginally significant effect (p < .10) on the relationship between production-related temporary employment usage and firm performance (ROI). However, the nature of the moderation is directly opposite of the one hypothesized. As reflected in figure 4 (with organization size held constant at its mean), production strategy moderates this relationship such that in a differentiation setting a positive relationship exists, and in a cost leadership setting a negative relationship exists. These results run contrary to the relationships proposed in hypothesis three (b). Note, however, that the moderation effects are marginally significant but extremely small, such that ROI changes very little. The slopes of the two lines in figure 4 are almost flat. With a beta coefficient of only –0.03, the interaction is marginally significant statistically, but it does not appear to affect ROI in any major fashion. These findings will be further discussed in the next chapter.

Table 11. Results of Regression Equation Three (b)

Dependent Variable: Performance	PERF	ROI
	Complete model beta coefficient	Complete model beta coefficient
Independent variable	(F=0.83, p=..52)	(F=6.19, p=.002)
Log of Employees (SIZE)	1.17	1.67***
Temp. Employee usage by Production Job Categories (PRODTEMP)	–0.24	0.19***
Product Strategy (PRODSTRAT)	–2.38	1.54*
Product X Temp. Usage (PRODTEMP X PRODSTRAT)	0.05	–0.03*
Constant	73.22***	–15.63***

***p<.01; **p<.05; *p<.10

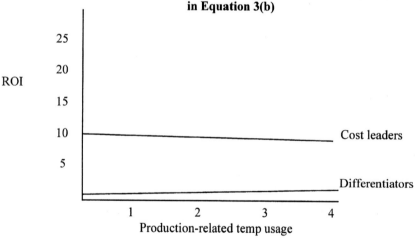

FIGURE 4

**Interaction of Production Strategy and
Production-Related Temporary Usage on Performance (ROI)
in Equation 3(b)**

Equation three (c) tested the moderating effect of marketing strategy on the relationship between overall temporary employee usage and organizational performance. Hypothesis three (c) stated that marketing strategy will moderate the temporary usage-performance linkage such that a positive relationship will exist in a breadth setting and a negative relationship will exist in a focus setting. Equation three (c) regressed organizational performance (PERF, ROI) on organization size (SIZE) in step one, on overall temporary employee usage (OVERTEMP) in step two, on marketing strategy (MKTSTRAT) in step three, and on the interaction between OVERTEMP and MKTSTRAT in step four. Hypothesis three (c) would be supported by significant incremental variance explained in step four (Cohen, 1968; Stone and Hollenbeck, 1984). With either PERF or ROI as the dependent variable, the interaction explained no significant variance (see table 12). Thus, hypothesis three (c) was not supported.

Equation three (d) regressed organizational performance (PERF, ROI) on organization size (SIZE) in step one, on marketing-related job category temporary use (MKTTEMP) in step two, on marketing strategy (MKTSTRAT) in step three, and on the interaction between MKTTEMP and MKTSTRAT in step four. Significant incremental variance explained in step four would support hypothesis three (d), that marketing strategy moderates the relationship between marketing-related temporary employment use and organizational performance such that a positive relationship will exist for breadth marketers and a negative relationship will exist for focus marketers (Cohen, 1968; Stone and Hollenbeck, 1984). Results showed that no significant variance was explained by any of the variables in either equation (see table 13). Thus, hypothesis three (d) was not supported.

Table 12. Hierarchical Regression Analysis, Equation Three (c)

Dependent Variable: Performance		PERF			ROI	
Independent variable	R^2	R^2 change	p of change	R^2	R^2 change	p of change
Step One: Log of Employees (SIZE)	.03	.03	.32	.11	.11	.09
Step Two: Log of Temp. employee usage (OVERTEMP)	.05	.02	.48	.19	.08	.14
Step Three: Marketing Strategy (MKTSTRAT)	.07	.02	.39	.21	.02	.50
Step Four: Market X temp. usage (OVERTEMP X MKTSTRAT)	.08	.01	.63	.21	.00	.79

Cumulative R^2 = 0.08
F = 0.61
p = 0.66
d.f. = 4, 28

Cumulative R^2 = 0.21
F = 1.43
p = 0.26
d.f. = 4, 21

Table 13. Hierarchical Regression Analysis, Equation Three (d)

Dependent Variable: Performance		PERF			ROI	
Independent variable	R^2	R^2 change	p of change	R^2	R^2 change	p of change
Step One:						
Log of Employees (SIZE)	.03	.03	.33	.11	.11	.10
Step Two:						
Temp. employee usage by Market Job Categories (MKTTEMP)	.03	.00	.89	.13	.02	.56
Step Three:						
Marketing Strategy (MKTSTRAT)	.05	.02	.44	.14	.01	.59
Step Four:						
Market X temp. usage (MKTTEMP X MKTSTRAT)	.05	.00	.86	.14	.00	.99

Cumulative R^2 = 0.05
F = 0.39
p = 0.81
d.f. = 4, 27

Cumulative R^2 = 0.14
F = 0.81
p = 0.53
d.f. = 4, 20

CHAPTER SEVEN

Discussion and Conclusions

DISCUSSION

Organizational strategy and temporary employment

Although the overall results of this study support only one of the eight hypotheses, several interesting insights may be pointed out. First, it is satisfying to note that the strategy data contained sufficient variability to suggest that organizations do indeed differ in their conscious choice of cost leadership or differentiation as well as focus or breadth. The production strategy data had a mean of 2.9 with a standard deviation of 1.5. The range of values was 0.3 to 6.0. The low average production strategy value represents an overall tendency toward differentiation rather than cost leadership within the sample. The marketing strategy variable had a mean of 5.5, a standard deviation of 1.4, and a range of 3.0 to 7.0. This high value indicates an overall tendency toward breadth as a marketing strategy in the study sample.

It appears that organizations may indeed be able to classify themselves on a continuum of strategic choice. The lack of results here may not be due to the strategy conceptualization, therefore, but may be related either to operationalizations of other variables in this study or to the lack of other variables being included in the research model. Of course, future empirical research should be undertaken to test the strategy typology approach more fully.

An examination of the mean values of the production- and marketing-related job category indices for temporary employees suggests one possibility for our lack of findings in marketing-related equations while some relationships were found when production-related data was used. Note that the mean value for the production-related temporary index is much higher (32.35%) than the mean value for the marketing-related temporary index (1.55%). It is noted that the marketing-related index was transformed to its square root for purposes of analysis. However, squaring the value, to 4%, still shows a major difference in the percentages of temporary employees utilized in production versus marketing job categories. As a much higher percentage of temporary employees appear to be employed in production-related jobs, it may be that these higher values may have influenced our ability to find significant relationships in the production-related regression equations pertaining to firm performance. In contrast, the low percentage of marketing-related temporary employment may have limited our ability to relate it to organizational performance.

This lower percentage of temporary employees working in sales and service positions is interesting on its own merits. As many of the companies included in the study sample were classified as service organizations, it would seem intuitive that larger numbers of temporaries in these firms would be classified into the sales and service categories. It is, therefore, highly probable that other marketing-related jobs exist outside the sales and service job categories. A significant percentage of jobs that are involved in marketing activities where temporaries may in fact be used may be classified into other job categories.

This finding highlights the probability that the type of organization will influence the nature and subsequent classification of jobs into particular job categories. Manufacturing companies will almost certainly have higher employment levels in manufacturing-related jobs, while service organizations will not. Service organizations necessarily have a different "production" process in which the product is intangible. Instead of employees who are involved in producing their companies' services being classified as operatives or laborers, they are more likely classified into other job categories such as professional or technical. The results of this study did not show that industry classification (manufacturing, service or other) was a significant factor in predicting the use of temporary employees. However, it appears that the job category operationalization may be too simplistic to capture differences among different firms based on industry. Future studies should include a more detailed investigation into job category classification based on industry.

The large discrepancy between marketing and production temporary employment levels may suggest two things. It may be that marketing-related jobs in general are less appropriate for the temporary employment arrangement. Marketing activities may involve more firm-specific knowledge, meaning that no matter how wide the market focus, employees involved in marketing a firm's product or service must be knowledgeable about its features.

Another possibility is that much of the marketing function may be outsourced to advertising or other marketing organizations whose core competencies allow them to effectively market clients' products or services for them. This outsourcing would not be classified as temporary employment in the manner that this study defines temporary employment. However, outsourcing is a type of contingent arrangement that is increasingly being utilized by today's organizations. Thus, outsourcing of marketing activities would not be reflected in this study's measure of temporary employment, but it represents an alternative work arrangement to permanent staffing. These are definitely interesting ideas that warrant further investigation in future research.

Organization size and other contextual variables

A factor that appears to have a complex relationship with temporary employment usage is organization size. Referring to the correlation matrix (table 3), SIZE, the survey's operationalization of organization size, is negatively correlated (-0.33, $p < .10$) with production-related temporary employment (PRODTEMP). The same marginally significant negative relationship exists with the two size proxies from the CompuStat data, SIZE-COMP ($r = -0.36$) and ASSETS ($r = -0.39$). Conversely, the SIZE variable from the survey is positively significantly correlated with MKTTEMP, the marketing-related temporary employment index ($r = 0.38$, $p < .05$). (SIZE-COMP and ASSETS did not have significant correlations with the MKT-TEMP variable.) Organization size, therefore, has a strong relationship with temporary usage in production and marketing jobs, but these relationships are in the opposite direction of one another.

The results of regression equations one (b) and two (b) also reveal this relationship. The beta value of SIZE in step one of equation one (b) is large and negative (-6.21, $p = .06$), denoting a negative effect of organization size on production-related temporary employee usage. Conversely, the beta value of SIZE when regressed on marketing-related temporary employee usage in step one of equation two (b) is positive (0.70) and highly significant ($p = .03$).

This suggests a more complex relationship between organization size and temporary employment than what was specified in this study. Organization size was not a significant control variable in the regressions pertaining to overall temporary employee usage [hypotheses 1(a) and 2(a)], but this could be a result of its directly opposite relationships with production- versus marketing-related temporary usage. The relationships would not be revealed in equations one (a) and two (a), as all temporary employment usage is combined into one value. However, by breaking temporary usage into different job "types" we find that the relationship between size and temporary employment may differ according to the strategic facet examined.

One possible explanation for the negative relationship between size and temporary usage in production-related positions is that, as an organization becomes larger, more permanent employees are available to "cover" for one another if a particular employee is scheduled to be out for an extended time period. In a smaller organization, however, a temporary employee may need to be brought in because others cannot be pulled away from their regular tasks. In other words, smaller organizations do not possess "slack" in their production processes in terms of human resources that larger organizations may have available to them. For example, one of the organizations in this sample, a small clothing manufacturer and distributor, cited as its top reason for using temporaries the "temporary replacement of absent employees." Most of its temporaries were utilized in distribution, which is part of the production process.

However, earlier research from structural contingency theory may provide more insight into these findings. Structural contingency theory assumes that organizations attempt to maximize the congruence or agreement between their structures and the context in which they do business (Perrow, 1970; Pfeffer, 1982). Contextual variables include, but are not limited to, size, technology, the environment, and strategy. Organizations alter their structures in relation to these variables. This study, for example, assumed that organizations would alter their work and job structures in order to be congruent with chosen competitive strategy.

Research regarding size as a variable affecting the structure of work in organizations has shown that, as size increases, work becomes more formalized and specialized (Blau, 1970; Child, 1972). In order to improve control over employee activities as the organization grows, bureaucracy is increased as division of labor becomes more prevalent, work roles become more formalized, and employees lose personal control over the work process (Blau, 1970; Pfeffer, 1982). Thus, overall, organization size influences the structure of work such that jobs become more structured as organizations become larger in order to more effectively monitor employee behaviors.

This would contradict the finding in this study, which shows that size is negatively related to the use of temporaries in production-related jobs. Jobs with more structure and formalized control would be assumed to be more appropriate for temporary employment than would jobs in smaller organizations that are less formalized and specialized. Smaller organizations will out of necessity allow employees more autonomy or personal control over their work activities, as they will have a broader range of tasks assigned to them.

The positive relationship between organization size and use of temporary employees in marketing-related job categories does reflect the earlier conception of the size-structure association. In marketing-related job categories, larger organizations may be better able to use temporaries because these jobs have become more specialized and formalized. For example, the positive relationship between size and temporary employee usage in marketing-related positions (i.e., sales and service) may reflect the ability of larger organizations to use temporaries such as telemarketers to market their products. Also, sales workers in the apparel industry that are hired as temporaries during peak seasons (i.e., the holidays) are likely utilized more by larger organizations than smaller ones. For example, two large retail organizations in the study sample, one with department/discount stores and one selling electronics, both reflected the majority of their temporary employment in the sales job category (75% and 85% respectively). These larger retail organizations likely have very formalized controls associated with narrowly defined marketing positions such as sales and telemarketing. Thus, temporary employees are able to step into these positions and satisfactorily carry out their assigned duties with minimal orientation and training.

The conflicting relationship of organization size with production- versus marketing-related temporary usage brings up broader issues regarding an organization's chosen structure. The question then becomes which contextual variables are more influential than others in particular organizational contexts, and which segments of the organization are most affected? If size, technology, the environment, and strategy are all considered to influence the subsequent structure that an organization adopts, does one or more of these variables affect structure more than the others? In this study, it was assumed that strategy is the most influential variable in an organization's chosen structure of work. Strategy was assumed to influence the technology used in the production process, as well as the structuring of marketing activities. This, in turn, was theorized to affect the nature of work needing to be accomplished and the structure of such work into jobs, which then influences transaction attributes of employment contracts. The nature of the employment contract was associated with the choice of using permanent or temporary employees, based on the structuring of tasks.

Instead, it was found in this study that organization size was more influential than was strategy in directly affecting temporary employment usage. Furthermore, the effect of size was not consistent across strategic facets (i.e., production versus marketing strategy). This brings up several important points. First, other contextual variables such as technology and the environment were not explicitly included in the research model. I assumed that strategy affected technology in a very simplistic manner, i.e., that cost leaders would adopt mechanized technology, while differentiators would adopt more complex, integrated technologies. This may not be the case, as technology such as advanced manufacturing, just-in-time and flexible manufacturing technologies are increasingly inexpensive to implement. Therefore, cost leaders as well as differentiators may adopt these technologies. Perhaps technology itself would better predict work structures than would strategy when examining the appropriateness of using temporary employees.

The influence of technology on organization structure is well documented (Woodward, 1965, 1970; Pfeffer, 1982). However, it may be that technology, especially in larger organizations, impacts more heavily only those units most intimately associated with the production process (Hickson, Pugh and Pheysey, 1969). Indeed, the attempt to link production strategy with temporary use in production-related job categories was meant to reflect this. As the organizations in the study tended to be large in size, this is a very important point. It may help to explain why technology, based on the choice of cost leadership or differentiation strategy, did not affect overall temporary employee usage. That is, the link between technology and overall work structures would be very weak in larger organizations. However, most important is the fact that the strategy operationalization does not appear to capture the nature of the sample organizations' technologies. Organizations classified in the manufacturing industry will necessarily utilize technologies much different than those used by service organizations, for instance. Future research regarding the influence of technologies may be more fruitful than strategic choice in investigating temporary employment levels.

Another important point is that the environment in which an organization exists may be highly influential on the structure of work processes (Burns and Stalker, 1961; Child, 1972). Organizations may choose more mechanized structures when operating in stable and certain environments, while others may utilize more organic (i.e., less formalized and centralized) structures if their environments are rapidly changing (Burns and Stalker, 1961).

To complicate things further, different organizational units may face different subenvironments that require different unit structures (Lawrence and Lorsch, 1967). Thus, investigation of organization structure becomes more complex as organizations become larger and divide into various units. Aggregate measures of structure may therefore be meaningless if structure varies by subunit (Pennings, 1973). The choice of level of analysis, therefore, is extremely important when assessing the influence of contextual variables on organization structure.

A last vital point regarding the structural contingency model is that, in many cases, measures of structure as well as contingency variables are obtained from individual organizational informants, as was the case in this study. Individuals may have differing perceptions about structure, strategy, the environment, or technology based on their particular work roles and experiences (Pennings, 1973). Therefore, any data obtained from individual informants will be filtered through perceptual processes. Furthermore, aggregation of individual perceptions may be highly inaccurate representations of organizational reality (Pennings, 1973).

The implication of this discussion for the current research study is that the research model does not take into account many contextual variables that may be highly influential in the structure of work within the sample organizations. A more complex model that includes technology, size, strategy, and the environment may improve the ability to predict specific work structures within organizations, which may then be linked to the use of temporary staffing. Future research should include these considerations.

Additionally, the use of individual informants in this research may mean that the data obtained in this study is not accurately representative of actual organization structure and strategy. A more complex study of the organizations' business units, work structures, technology and so on should be undertaken in order to obtain objective information about the contexts in which the target companies exist.

However, from a structural contingency perspective, it is satisfying to note that the findings of this study reflect interactional effects of the strategy contingency variable and the temporary employment structural variable in predicting firm performance. When making predictions about organizations adapting to their contexts, one is explicitly specifying an interaction (Pfeffer, 1982; Schoonhoven, 1981). The adaptation of organization structure to context is assumed in structural contingency theory to enhance organizational effectiveness. In this study, two significant interactions within the results may serve as some evidence supporting the mutual relationship between context and structure.

In the research study, two interactions were found to be significant. Equation three (a) produced the desired results for the subjective performance index (PERF), that the production strategy/temporary usage interaction was significant and reflected the hypothesized moderating effect. The main effects of temporary employee usage (OVERTEMP) and production strategy (PRODSTRAT) are large and negative, while the interaction term is large and positive. This interaction is consistent with the hypothesized moderating effect of production strategy on temporary employee usage and firm performance. When temporary usage and production strategy "agree," the effects of the interaction on performance are positive. The interaction is shown in figure 3. These findings support predictions made in this study regarding the fit between temporary employee use and strategy.

It is noted that an opposite moderating effect of production strategy on ROI and temporary employment was reflected in equation three (b), which restricted the temporary employment measure to production-related job categories (PRODTEMP). The interaction is pictured in figure 4. A relationship opposite of that hypothesized is reflected. The interaction is marginally significant, although in reality the effect is small when plotted as in figure 4. However, cost leaders appear to experience lessened performance as they utilize more temporary employees, while differentiators tend to enjoy greater performance as they use more temporary employees in production-related jobs. This directly conflicts with the model put forth in this study.

The contrasting findings have a plausible explanation. The subjective performance index developed from the survey included non-accounting performance components such as quality and service. These areas of performance would not necessarily have a positive impact on the organizational bottom line, but may instead be more costly in an accounting sense in that they take more time and effort. On the other hand, ROI only includes accounting-based numbers and would thus reflect organizational activities that are cost-saving in nature.

Intuitively, it makes sense that while the use of temporary employees may be cheaper and thus would have a positive impact on ROI, the use of such employees may negatively impact areas such as quality or service. Similarly, firms may save money by operating as cost leaders rather than differentiators, which would positively impact ROI, while quality and service would not be emphasized and would thus be given lower subjective performance ratings.

Indeed, if we examine table 11, where ROI is used as the dependent variable, we see that both production strategy and production-related temporary usage reflect some of these effects. The index of temporaries in production-related job categories (PRODTEMP) has a highly significant beta coefficient of 0.19 ($p < .01$), reflecting a positive effect of production temporary use on ROI. Additionally, the beta coefficient for the production strategy variable (PRODSTRAT) is 1.54, which is marginally significant ($p < .10$). This positive effect indicates that as firms become more cost-leader oriented, ROI is positively impacted.

Conversely, note the results in table 9 when subjective performance (PERF) is the dependent variable. Both the overall use of temporary employees (OVERTEMP) and production strategy (PRODSTRAT) exhibit extremely significant ($p < .01$) beta coefficients that are large and negative (-15.30 and −12.58 respectively). This tells us that as organizations use more temporaries and as firms tend toward heavier cost leadership, subjective performance suffers. It is entirely possible that areas like customer service and quality are negatively impacted when more temporaries are used and as firms move away from differentiation tactics.

It is intuitively appealing to suggest that although temporary employment use and cost leader-oriented product strategy may negatively impact subjective performance ratings directly, at least when the use of temporary employees is more appropriate as in the cost leadership setting the interaction somewhat mitigates the negative main effects. However, if we were to apply the same logic to the regression equation three (b) interaction when ROI is the dependent variable, our argument for "fit" between strategy and temp usage appears opposite of what is theorized here. Of course, future research should address this inconsistency.

LIMITATIONS

Several limitations exist in this study. First, the sample size of firms was small. Every effort was made to assure that firms participated in the study. However, these efforts did not increase response rate appreciably.

The low response rate could be a function of several factors. Many organizations declined to participate due to company policy or to lack of time resulting from heavy workloads. As the organizations probably receive numerous requests for research participation, this is not surprising. The target sample for the present study is a popular one for survey mailouts.

However, and perhaps most important, is the fact that several organizations communicated that although they would be very interested in participating, their organizations simply did not have records regarding their temporary employment use. Some of these organizations were in the process of restructuring their record-keeping and reporting responsibilities regarding temporary employment. Perhaps the importance of temporary employment is just now reaching the critical point at which organizations want to start tracking its effectiveness, which had not been previously done in many cases. If few organizations have centralized records of temporary employee usage, this is certainly a possible explanation for the major lack of response to the survey.

If the lack of records regarding temporary employment is a widespread phenomenon, this creates obvious difficulties for the study of temporary staffing. It is not known exactly how many of the organizations that declined to participate did so because of lack of centralized information regarding temporary employment. This is in itself a very important area to be researched. The HR practitioners to whom I spoke seemed particularly interested in the results of this study and communicated their interest in the study of temporary employment in general. Therefore, a lack of centralized records is probably not due to disinterest. In any case, future research into the availability of data regarding temporary employment would be extremely useful.

The choice of the Hoover's Handbook (1996) as the target sample turned out to be somewhat problematic. As the handbook includes larger organizations, this limited the usefulness of the sample for the present study. As previously discussed, larger organizations tend to be more complex in structure, such that direct relationships between overall organizational structure and contingency variables are difficult to study. For example, the relatively high value of the marketing strategy variable may be a factor in our lack of findings. Its mean value of 5.5, on a seven-point scale, tells us that organizations in the sample have chosen relatively broad customer markets. This is easy to understand, as the sample was drawn from the population of very large organizations contained in the Hoover's Handbook (1996). Larger firms may naturally have to market to wider customer bases in order to create the necessary demand for their products or services. The absence of smaller organizations in this study's sample may unduly restrict the marketing strategy variable's ability to vary.

Additionally, as organizations become larger, they organize into distinct units. Again, as discussed in an earlier section, this creates difficulties with the choice of level of analysis for study. A reflection of this is in the present study. It is highly likely that the use of the business strategy concept while surveying organizations at the corporate level has caused problems in finding significant relationships in this study. A more appropriate method of investigating the link between business strategy and temporary employee usage would include unit-level measures of performance, temporary employee usage, and strategy. This level of data was not obtained but should be gathered in the future.

An additional limitation of the research study is that survey methodology can result in common method variance due to single respondents from each client firm. This may introduce sizeable error in the measurement of HR practices, organizational strategy and performance in this study (Gerhart, 1999). Consequently reliabilities could be quite low, which will affect the accuracy of results and conclusions drawn from such results (Gerhart, 1999). Single-response research can also introduce spuriously high relationships between variables, as a respondent may allow responses on some items to influence other responses. However, we did not see many significant relationships among the variables in this study, so this problem may not be as large as other existing limitations.

As noted, two surveys were sent to each responding organization in an attempt to combat this problem. This is a large limitation to the present study, as only one organization returned two useable responses. The only available check on the survey data was the CompuStat data collected for publicly traded firms within the study sample, and this information was limited. Therefore, many of the variables obtained from the survey could not be cross-checked. More extensive studies are needed to further investigate any tentative conclusions drawn from this survey information.

An additional need is to conduct more in-depth case studies of organizations in order to further understand the effects of contingency variables such as strategy as well as firm idiosyncracies on strategic HR activities and firm performance (Becker and Gerhart, 1996). Follow-up communication with the participating organizations of this study should be undertaken regarding possible further research into their use of temporary employment. It is hoped that their initial willingness to take part in the research signals participating organizations' interest in learning more about the effectiveness of their temporary employment usage.

Another difficulty is the very nature of perceptual measures of strategy. It may be that HR managers in general understand strategic imperatives, but their perceptions may be restricted to the particular segment of the organization with which they are familiar. In any case, instead of using per ceptual measures of strategic imperatives that may be inaccurate representations of organization strategy, it will be more useful in future studies to obtain objective strategy measures through archival market information (e.g., the entropy measure, Jacquemin and Berry, 1979) or for researchers to personally study business units in a qualitative fashion and to make strategy determinations independent of organizational informant perceptions.

Referring to the data in this study regarding strategy, results show no support for either production or marketing strategy having a significant effect on temporary employment usage, either overall or in particular job categories. One factor is that it may be the strategy variable operationalizations were not adequately representative of the production and marketing strategy facets. The initial difficulty in obtaining reasonable internal consistency values for the strategy values was an early indication that this may be the case. It was discussed earlier that Porter's typology, along with other strategic typologies, may not capture the true essence of an organization's strategy (Chadwick and Cappelli, 1999). It appears that a more complex operationalization may indeed be needed in future research if we are to find relationships between firm strategy and temporary employment.

On the other hand, it may be that the use of strategic typologies in general is not the best method of studying organizational strategy (Chadwick and Cappelli, 1999). As previously noted in this research, strategy has of late been described as a much more complex phenomenon than can be captured by simplistic typologies. We should follow closely the progress of researchers trying to operationalize strategy in a richer way, and we should then apply the results of that future research in the SHRM arena.

The use of job-category employment may not provide a robust measure of strategy-related job activities. It may be that job categories are not as homogeneous as initially assumed, and so do not give enough detail about the structure of jobs within organizations. Furthermore, the use of job categories to reflect production- and marketing-related activities did not appear to capture the complex nature of organization structure in the sample organizations. Future qualitative investigation may shed light on more meaningful characterizations of temporary employment at the job level.

The subjective-objective performance debate is also evident in the study's performance operationalizations. It is still not clear whether subjective or objective performance is a superior representation of underlying true organization performance. Accounting performance is important, as organizational stakeholders constantly monitor profits and returns. However, accounting measures are recognized as being subject to distortion at times. So, organizational researchers constantly seek newer and better representations of "true" performance, incorporating more subjective aspects of organizational outcomes. For example, a new way of measuring performance in a strategic fashion is advocated by Kaplan and Norton

(1992, 1996). A so-called "balanced scorecard" of performance areas including financial, customer, internal business processes, and learning and growth may be developed to allow organizations to monitor specific activities that support strategic direction. Financial outcomes remain important, but organizations are encouraged to identify underlying causes for improved financial numbers such as increased market share or customer satisfaction (customer dimension), quality (internal business processes dimension), or improved employee capabilities (learning and growth dimension). Each organization chooses the performance areas that are most closely linked to achieving strategic goals (Kaplan and Norton, 1996).

This trend toward deeper and more organization-specific analysis of firm performance is a fruitful area for future research. It may provide a useful alternative to commonly used accounting measures such as ROI or ROA. However, its qualitative nature may preclude its use in survey-based research. This is an empirical question, of course, that needs to be addressed.

The cross-sectional nature of the present study is also a limitation to its usefulness. If we are to understand the effectiveness of temporary employment use, we will likely need longer-term research in order to assess trends over time in temporary use. An increase of temporary employment levels over a several-year period will likely provide us with deeper insight into its effectiveness. Fluctuations in temporary employee levels could lead us to examine the underlying reasons why these levels change over time. Do organizations find that temporary employment provides value, and thus levels are increased? Or does overuse of temporary employees tend to erode competitive advantage, such that levels are decreased?

Other influences on the use of temporary employment may also be unearthed, such as labor market changes, or the use of temporaries to lower fixed human capital costs in reports to shareholders. In other words, external pressures such as labor market characteristics or "non-rational" activities on part of management may impact temporary employee usage. A longitudinal case study of several organizations would provide much richer information about the decision-making process that strategic human resource managers go through in setting or adjusting temporary employment levels.

The restriction of this study to only studying a particular type of contingent staffing, temporary employment, is a limitation but one that was felt to be very necessary. A comprehensive program of research over time needs to be undertaken that includes the study of all types of contingent work. Outsourcing of particular activities or use of independent contractor arrangements, for instance, may be effective employment arrangements for particular strategic contingencies. It will take time to build such a research program, but it is an important area of research to address.

It is recognized that other factors influence the linkages proposed in the research model, such that a fully specified model has not been developed. However, the complex nature of firms usually precludes fully specified models in any organizational research. Information gleaned from this study is worthwhile in that it provides further insight into a specific area of the complex organization, that of the strategic use of temporary staffing.

Finally, a general lack of findings may also be attributable to the fact that many factors exist in organizations that affect human resource activities as well as firm performance. It was discussed earlier that structural contingency theory identifies many other contextual variables that influence the nature of work in organizations (Pfeffer, 1982). It has been noted that SHRM researchers may have difficulties showing that human resource activities affect firm outcomes because so many factors are simultaneously at work (Gerhart, 1999). It may be somewhat presumptuous for us to believe that human resource activities have a strong enough effect on firm outcomes that we will find significant HR predictors in our SHRM models. HR activities are a part of a larger whole, the organization itself, so significant results may be difficult to find.

Furthermore, when we do find significance, we should interpret with caution. Prior research in the area of SHRM has been criticized for its normative nature. In other words, SHRM theory assumes that the use of particular HR activities in specific organizational settings will naturally result in more effective performance. It ignores the concept of equifinality, which says that there are countless ways for firms to organize internally (Chadwick and Cappelli, 1999). Additionally, structural contingency theory purports that there is no one best way to organize (Galbraith, 1973). This presents problems when attempting to link particular HR activities or patterns of HR activities with strategy in influencing organizational effectivness. It may be that "strategy" itself is an organization-specific notion. Each organization has a complex set of contingencies, including strategy, size, technology, industry and environment, and so on. Furthermore, implementation of various organizational structures and programs is executed by managers who interpret context in individual ways.

Therefore, theories of SHRM may need to move away from normative prescriptions of the "best way to organize" and instead focus on individual organizations and their needs. Use of the resource-based view of the firm (Barney, 1991) in concert with organization-specific data regarding structure, technology, the environment, and subsequent work structures may be much more valuable to the area of SHRM in the future. It may aid us in understanding the manner in which organizations adapt themselves to numerous interactive contextual concerns.

CONCLUSIONS

Conclusions drawn from this research study may only be considered tentative, due to the numerous limitations cited in the previous section.

However, a few interesting findings may be noted. Although we did not find significant direct effects of competitive strategy on the use of temporary employment, it seems that the interaction of these two variables does indeed impact firm performance. However, the direction of interaction may depend upon the choice of firm performance measure, being either subjective or objective in nature.

Therefore, it appears that before we attempt to link HR activities with firm performance, we need to determine which definition of performance is best for our particular research question. If cost reduction is a goal of an HR imperative, then we will likely look for an improvement in accounting performance. However, if an HR activity is undertaken in order to improve a more esoteric performance dimension, for example customer service, the impact on accounting performance may not be significant. We would instead need to examine the qualitative performance dimension of customer satisfaction. In other words, we will need to be more specific in our definitions of performance based on the research question at hand.

It is important to extend this work in the future through more in-depth case studies of organizations and their use of temporaries. It appears that the relationships between strategy and temporary employment are more complex. Therefore, survey methodology may not be the most effective manner of study for these phenomena. On the other hand, the adequacy of survey methodology may rely totally on the organization's ability to provide the requested information. In this study, perhaps the inability of many firms to provide comprehensive information about their temporary employment usage is the largest factor in the lack of findings here. Furthermore, the data regarding strategic imperatives may be assessed more accurately through information from top-level managers as well as from outside data. We will indeed require richer information in future research, which can only be obtained through qualitative research methodology. However, survey methodology can complement such qualititative research in most instances.

This brings up the fact that organizational research is becoming less and less compartmentalized. Instead of strategy researchers working independently from human resource researchers, findings from all areas are becoming more interdependent. The consequence of this is that strategic HR researchers must now be conversant in not only the HR literature, but also literature from the areas of strategic management, finance, accounting, economics, industrial/organizational psychology, sociology, and so on. By the same token, it is hoped that researchers in these other areas recognize the importance of human resource management when undertaking research in their areas. Research of an interdisciplinary nature can be very rewarding and insightful.

We also recognize that organizations are much more complex than in the past. In addition to the traditional hierarchical view that we have taken of firms in the past, these organizations now have alternatives to the traditional structure. The tremendous growth in the area of contingent employment is a result of organizations recognizing that outsourcing and contract arrangements may be more beneficial than the traditional employment arrangement. The "network" organization, in which groups of firms work together with each contributing its particular core competencies, is a common form of the more modern organization. This is requiring organizational researchers to utilize more qualitative forms of investigation in order to flesh out the idiosyncracies and complexities that are particular to individual firms.

Several contributions of this study exist. First, it has integrated streams of research from the areas of strategic human resource management, strategic management and industrial economics to develop a theoretical basis for the strategic use of temporary employees. The transaction cost economics framework is one that lends itself quite well to the decision-making process of internalization or externalization of employment. By integrating transaction cost theory with strategic management concepts, the research provides a way of examining the strategic staffing question from a theory-based standpoint.

Next, the responses to the survey provided some support to the notion that HR managers are thinking more strategically and are more involved in the strategic development of the organization. The HR managers with whom I had contact expressed their great interest in results of the study. They also communicated their heightened awareness of the strategic management process within their organizations. We should see an increase in this trend of HR managers taking part in strategic planning and implementation in the future. These HR managers may then be more valuable sources of information regarding their perceptions of the effectiveness of strategically managing HR activities.

The limited results of the study have pointed out that the new conceptualizations of organizational strategy and performance are still in their infancy. The difficulties of operationalizing qualitative aspects of firm activities are continually being addressed. Future empirical research into the complexity in the areas of the resource-based view of the firm (Barney, 1991), strategic human resource management (Chadwick and Cappelli, 1999; Gerhart, 1999; Becker and Gerhart, 1996), and even firm performance (Kaplan and Norton, 1992, 1996) will hopefully give us a clearer picture of qualitative differences across firms that must be addressed.

The significant findings of this research study do suggest that relationships exist between human resource activities and strategic contingencies that impact the organizational bottom-line. Of course, the conflicting findings based on the operationalization of performance provide a challenge for future research. This conflict provides a contribution to the SHRM literature because it points out that we must be very careful to fully define our performance objectives. We cannot ignore the complexities of organizational performance and must choose the measure that is appropriate for the research at hand.

Finally, it is hoped that this study has contributed to the field of strategic human resource management by explicitly pointing out that strategic staffing cannot be assumed to always involve internal, permanent employment. Strategic staffing research must address the fact that other forms of employment do exist, and these different employment arrangements may or may not be appropriate for each organization. If we are to understand which forms of employment arrangements are effective for particular organizations, we must study the linkages of the different arrangements to strategic imperatives. We may then be able to aid human resource managers in their decision-making processes about staffing arrangements that are appropriate to their strategic situations.

Appendix A
Survey

THE STRATEGIC USE OF TEMPORARY EMPLOYMENT

This is a survey asking you about your general use of temporary employees in your organization. Your individual responses and your organization's identity will be kept **completely confidential** by the researcher.

Thank you for your participation.

This survey should take you about **20 minutes** to complete.

Part I Organizational description

Currently, how many full-time employees work in your organization?_____

What is your position?_____

How long have you held this position?_____

In what industry does the majority of your
organization's sales occur?_____

What is your principal product or service?_____

What percentage of your company's employees
are <u>unionized</u>?   0%   10   20   30   40   50   60   70   80   90   100%

Does your company utilize temporary employees? _____ Yes _____ No

If no, please explain: _____
(then go on to Part III)

_____

Part II Reasons for using temporaries

Following is a list of ten possible reasons for using temporary employees. Please indicate what you consider your **three most** important and **three least** important reasons for using temporaries by writing in the blank beside the corresponding reason a 1, 2, or 3 where 1 is the most important, and 8, 9, or 10 where 10 is the least important. (Four items will be left blank.)

_____ Lack of availability of job applicants with necessary skills

_____ Lower wage costs

_____ Avoidance of benefits and overhead costs

_____ Following trend of industry competitors

_____ Avoidance of possible litigation, such as wrongful discharge suits

_____ Parent company limits employee headcounts

_____ Avoidance of union problems

_____ Outsourcing to fill non-core business needs

_____ Flexibility in manufacturing output

_____ Flexibility in employee levels

Part III Extent of temporary usage

(Please answer any items that apply.) What approximate percentage of your organization's <u>total</u> annual labor hours do you estimate were worked by temporary employees:

1. in the past year?   _____ %

2. five years ago?   _____ %

3. Your projection for
   five years from now?   _____ %

Manufacturing:	_____ %		Manufacturing:	_____ %
Marketing:	_____ %		Marketing:	_____ %
Planning/design:	_____ %		Planning/design:	_____ %
Sales/service:	_____ %		Sales/service:	_____ %
Operations	_____ %		Operations	_____ %
Engineering/projects	_____ %		Engineering/projects	_____ %
Maintenance	_____ %		Maintenance	_____ %
Administrative	_____ %		Administrative	_____ %
Finance	_____ %		Finance	_____ %
Programming	_____ %		Programming	_____ %
Research	_____ %		Research	_____ %
MIS	_____ %		MIS	_____ %

Other (please specify):   Other (please specify):

_____ _____ %   _____ _____ %

_____ _____ %   _____ _____ %

                    Total   100 %   Total   100 %

Managerial	_____ %
Professional	_____ %
Technical	_____ %
Sales	_____ %
Clerical	_____ %
Craft worker	_____ %

How was your organization's <u>total</u> level of <u>employment</u> divided across <u>departments</u> in the past year, including temporaries? (Total should sum to 100%.)

Operative	_____ %
Laborer	_____ %
Service	_____ %

Other (please specify):

_____   _____ %

_____   _____ %

           Total   100 %

Managerial	_____ %
Professional	_____ %
Technical	_____ %
Sales	_____ %
Clerical	_____ %
Craft worker	_____ %

How was your organization's use of <u>temporaries</u> divided across <u>departments</u> in the past year? (Total should sum to 100%.)

Operative	_____ %
Laborer	_____ %
Service	_____ %

Other (please specify):

_____   _____ %

_____   _____ %

           Total   100 %

Part IV Assessment of industry environment

	Not at all			Somewhat		Very	
How <u>stable</u> would you rate your industry?	1	2	3	4	5	6	7
How <u>frequently</u> does the relevant <u>technology</u> in your industry <u>change</u>?	1	2	3	4	5	6	7
How <u>intense</u> is market <u>competition</u> in your industry?	1	2	3	4	5	6	7
How <u>cyclical</u> or <u>seasonal</u> is demand for <u>employees</u> in your industry?	1	2	3	4	5	6	7

How was your organization's <u>total</u> level of <u>employment</u> divided across <u>job categories</u> in the past year, including temporaries? (Total should sum to 100%.)

How was your organization's use of <u>temporaries</u> divided in the past year? (Total should sum to 100%.)

Part V
Firm/division performance

Consider the performance of your firm or division relative to your competitors in your industry. How would you rate your performance relative to these competitors on:

Operating Efficiency	Bottom 10%	Bottom 20%	Bottom 30%	Bottom 40%	Average 50%	Top 40%	Top 30%	Top 20%	Top 10%
Quality	Bottom 10%	Bottom 20%	Bottom 30%	Bottom 40%	Average 50%	Top 40%	Top 30%	Top 20%	Top 10%
Service	Bottom 10%	Bottom 20%	Bottom 30%	Bottom 40%	Average 50%	Top 40%	Top 30%	Top 20%	Top 10%
Sales	Bottom 10%	Bottom 20%	Bottom 30%	Bottom 40%	Average 50%	Top 40%	Top 30%	Top 20%	Top 10%
Profitability	Bottom 10%	Bottom 20%	Bottom 30%	Bottom 40%	Average 50%	Top 40%	Top 30%	Top 20%	Top 10%
Market Share	Bottom 10%	Bottom 20%	Bottom 30%	Bottom 40%	Average 50%	Top 40%	Top 30%	Top 20%	Top 10%

Part VI Your firm's competitive strategy *

Where does the price of your organization's major product or service stand in relation to competitors?

Significantly lower						Significantly higher
1	2	3	4	5	6	7

Is your major product/service designed to appeal to everyone, or is your product/service designed with special features that appeal to a narrow audience willing to pay more for it?

Wide audience						Narrow audience
1	2	3	4	5	6	7

To what extent does your firm concentrate your marketing efforts on a specific geographic or consumer market, relative to your industry competitors?

Significantly more concentrated						Significantly less concentrated
1	2	3	4	5	6	7

To what extent does your firm utilize mass marketing, relative to your industry competitors?

Significantly more						Significantly less
1	2	3	4	5	6	7

What percentage of your company's sales are accounted for by low-cost, generic products or services?

0%   10   20   30   40   50   60   70   80   90   100%

What percentage of your company's sales are accounted for by "high performance" products or services?

0%   10   20   30   40   50   60   70   80   90   100%

To what extent is your organization's major product or service considered to be "more expensive, but worth the price" in relation to your competitors?

Not so at all						Very much so
1	2	3	4	5	6	7

How widely distributed is your organization's major product or service?

Locally		Regionally		Nationally		Internationally
1	2	3	4	5	6	7

How well is your organization's major product or service known or recognized by the general public?

Locally		Regionally		Nationally		Internationally
1	2	3	4	5	6	7

* If any of the above items about competitive strategy do not pertain to your organization, please explain:

_____

_____

_____

_____

_____

_____

_____

Thank you for taking the time to complete this important questionnaire. If you would like to receive a summary of the overall results, please indicate where you would like it to be sent.

Name

_____

Company

_____

Address

_____

_____

Your response to this survey is very important. Please return it promptly.

Please return this questionnaire in the enclosed postage paid envelope.

Thank you!

References

Abraham, K.G. 1988. Flexible staffing arrangements and employers' short-term adjustment strategies. In Robert A. Hart (ed.), *Employment, Unemployment, and Labor Utilization*, 288–311. London: Unwin Hyman.

Alchian, A.A. and Demsetz, H. 1972. Production, information cost, and economic organization. *American Economic Review*, 62: 777–795.

Arthur, J.B. 1992. The link between business strategy and industrial relations systems in American steel minimills. *Industrial and Labor Relations Review*, 45: 488–506.

Arthur, J.B. 1994. Effects of human resource systems on manufacturing performance and turnover. *Academy of Management Journal*, 37: 670–687.

Autor, D.H. 2000. Outsourcing at will: Unjust dismissal doctrine and the growth of temporary help employment. http://web.mit.edu/dautor/www/EAWFeb2000.pdf.

Barney, J.B. 1991. Firm resources and sustained competitive advantage. *Journal of Management*, 17: 99–120.

Baron, J.N., Davis-Blake, A. and Bielby W.T. 1986. The structure of opportunity: how promotion ladders vary within and among organizations. *Administrative Science Quarterly*, 31: 248–273.

Beard, D.W. and Dess, G.G. 1981. Corporate-level strategy, business-level strategy and firm performance. *Academy of Management Journal*, 24: 663–688.

Becker, B. and Gerhart, B. 1996. The impact of human resource management on organizational performance: Progress and prospects. *Academy of Management Journal*, 39: 779–801.

Becker, G. 1962. Investment in human capital: a theoretical analysis. *Journal of Political Economy*, supplement, 70: 9–44.

Belous, R. 1989. *The Contingent Economy: The Growth of the Temporary, Part-Time and Subcontracted Workforce*. Washington, D.C.: National Planning Association.

Blau, P.M. 1970. A formal theory of differentiation in organizations. *American Sociological Review*, 35: 201–218.

Bureau of Labor Statistics. 1999. Contingent and alternative employment arrangements, February 1999. http://stats.bls.gov/newsrels.htm.

Burns, T. and Stalker, G.M. 1961. *The Management of Innovation.* London: Tavistock.

Butler, J.E., Ferris, G.R., and Napier, N.K. 1991. *Strategy and Human Resources Management.* Cincinnati, OH: South-Western Publishing Co.

Campbell, D. and Fiske, D. 1959. Convergent and discriminant validation by the multitrait-multimethod matrix. *Psychological Bulletin*, 56: 81–105.

Cappelli, P. and Singh, H. 1992. Integrating strategic human resources and strategic management. In D. Lewin, O.S. Mitchell and P. Shere (Eds.), *Research Frontiers in Industrial Relations and Human Resources*, 165–192. Madison, WI: Industrial Relations Research Association.

Caudron, S. 1994a. Contingent work force spurs HR planning. *Personnel Journal*, July 1994, 52–60.

Caudron, S. 1994b. Calculating the cost of contingent workers. *Personnel Journal*, November 1994, 48A-48C.

Chadwick, C. and Cappelli, P., 1999. Alternatives to generic strategy typologies in strategic human resource management. In G.R. Ferris (Ed.), *Research in Personnel and Human Resources Management*, Vol. 18, Supplement 4, *Strategic Human Resources Management in the Twenty-First Century*, P.M. Wright, L.D. Dyer and J.W. Boudreau (eds.). Greenwich, CT: JAI Press.

Child, J. 1972. Organizational structure, environment and performance: the role of strategic choice. *Sociology*, 6: 1–22.

Coase, R.H. 1937. The nature of the firm. *Economica*, 4: 386–405.

Cohen, J. 1968. Multiple regression as a general data-analytic system. *Psychological Bulletin*, 70: 426–443.

Cohen, Y. and Pfeffer, J. 1986. Organizational hiring standards. *Administrative Science Quarterly*, 31: 1–24.

Cooper, S.F. 1995. The expanding use of the contingent workforce in the American economy: new opportunities and dangers for employers. *Employee Relations Law Journal*, 20: 525–539.

Cronbach, L. 1951. Coefficient alpha and the internal structure of tests. *Psychometrika*, 16: 297–334.

Davis-Blake, A. and Uzzi, B. 1993. Determinants of employment externalization: a study of temporary workers and independent contractors. *Administrative Science Quarterly*, 38: 195–223.

Dean, J.W., Jr. and Snell, S.A. 1991. Integrated manufacturing and job design: moderating effects of organizational inertia. *Academy of Management Journal*, 34: 776–804.

Delaney, J.T. and Huselid, M.A. 1996. The impact of human resource management practices on perceptions of organizational performance. *Academy of Management Journal*, 39: 949–969.

Eisenhardt, K.M. 1989. Agency theory: an assessment and review. *Academy of Management Review*, 14: 57–74.

Fama, E.F. and Jensen, M.C. 1983. Separation of ownership and control. *Journal of Law and Economics*, 26: 301–325.

Galbraith, J. 1973. *Designing Complex Organizations*. Reading, MA: Addison-Wesley.

Gerhart, B. 1999. Human resource management and firm performance: challenges in making causal inferences. In G.R. Ferris (Ed.), *Research in Personnel and Human Resources Management*, Vol. 18, Supplement 4, *Strategic Human Resources Management in the Twenty-First Century*, P.M. Wright, L.D. Dyer and J.W. Boudreau (eds.). Greenwich, CT: JAI Press.

Greene, W.H. 1993. *Econometric Analysis* (third edition). New York: Macmillan Publishing Company.

Gupta, A.K. and Govindarajan, V. 1984. Business unit strategy, managerial characteristics, and business unit effectiveness at strategy implementation. *Academy of Management Journal*, 27: 25–41.

Guthrie, J.P. and Olian, J.D. 1991. Does context affect staffing decisions? The case of general managers. *Personnel Psychology*, 44: 263–292.

Guthrie, J.P., Grimm, C.M. and Smith, K.G. 1991. Environmental change and management staffing: an empirical study. *Journal of Management*, 17: 735–748.

Herer, Y.T. and G.H. Harel. 1998. Determining the size of the temporary workforce—an inventory modeling approach. *Human Resource Planning*, 21: 20–32.

Hickson, D.J., Pugh, D.S. and Pheysey, D.C. 1969. Operations technology and organization structure: an empirical reappraisal. *Administrative Science Quarterly*, 14: 378–397.

Hoover's Handbook of American Business 1996. P.J. Spain and J.R. Talbot (Eds.). Austin, TX: The Reference Press, Inc.

Houseman, S.N. 1999. *Futurework: Trends and challenges for work in the 21st century*. http://www.dol.gov/dol/asp/public/futurework/conference/staffing/staffing.

Jackson, S.E., Schuler, R.S. and Rivero, J.C. 1989. Organizational characteristics as predictors of personnel practices. *Personnel Psychology*, 42: 727–786.

Jacobson, R. 1987. The validity of ROI as a measure of business performance. *American Economic Review*, 77: 470–478.

Jacquemin, A.P. and Berry, C.H. 1979. Entropy measure of diversification and corporate growth. *Journal of Industrial Economics*, 27: 359–369.

Jensen, M.C. and Meckling, W.H. 1976. Theory of the firm: managerial behavior, agency costs, and ownership structure. *Journal of Financial Economics*, 3: 305–360.

Jones, G.R. 1984. Task visibility, free riding, and shirking: explaining the effect of structure and technology on employee behavior. *Academy of Management Review*, 9: 684–695.

Jones, G.R. and Wright, P.M. 1992. An economic approach to conceptualizing the utility of human resource management practices. *Research in Personnel and Human Resources Management*, 10: 271–299.

Kahn, S. and Foulkes, F. 1995. Human resource challenges of the burgeoning temporary workforce: findings from a survey of human resource managers. Paper presented at the Academy of Management meetings, Vancouver B.C., August 1995.

Kaplan, R.S. and D.P. Norton 1992. The balanced scorecard: measures that drive performance. *Harvard Business Review*, 70: 71–79.

Kaplan, R.S. and D.P. Norton 1996. Linking the balanced scorecard to strategy. *California Management Review*, 39: 53–79.

Kerlinger, F.N. 1986. *Foundations of Behavioral Research*, 3rd edition. Fort Worth, TX: Holt, Rinehart and Winston, Inc.

Kerr, J.L. and Jackofsky, E.F. 1989. Aligning mangers with strategies: management development versus selection. *Strategic Management Journal*, 10: 157–170.

Khojasteh, M. 1994. Workforce 2000: demographic changes and their impacts. *International Journal of Public Administration*, 17: 465–505.

Lawrence, P. and Lorsch, J. 1967. *Organization and Environment*. Homewood, IL: Irwin.

Lohtia, R., Brooks, C.M. and Krapfel, R.E. 1994. What constitutes a transaction-specific asset? An examination of the dimensions and types. *Journal of Business Research*, 30: 261–270.

Mangum, G., Mayall, D. and Nelson, K. 1985. The temporary help industry: a response to the dual internal labor market. *Industrial and Labor Relations Review*, 38: 599–611.

McClave, J.T. and Benson, P.G. 1988. *Statistics for Business and Economics* (fourth edition). San Francisco, CA: Dellen Publishing Company.

Micco, L. 1999. Employment in the 21st century. *Bulletin to Management*, November 25, 1999, pp. S1–S4. Washington, D.C.: Bureau of National Affairs, Inc.

Miles, R. and Snow, C. 1978. *Organization Strategy, Structure, and Process*. New York, NY: McGraw-Hill.

Nollen, S.D. and Axel, H. 1996. Benefits and costs to employers. In K.B. Barker and K. Christensen (eds.), *Contingent Work: American Employment Relations in Transition*, pp. 126–143. Ithaca, NY: Cornell University Press.

Ouchi, W.G. 1980. Markets, bureaucracies and clans. *Administrative Science Quarterly*, 25: 129–141.

Pearce, J.L. 1993. Toward an organizational behavior of contract laborers: their psychological involvement and effects on employee co-workers. *Academy of Management Journal*, 36: 1082–1096.

Pennings, J.M. 1973. Measures of organizational structure: A methodological note. *American Journal of Sociology*, 79: 686–704.

Perrow, C. 1970. *Organizational Analysis: A Sociological View*. Belmont, CA: Wadsworth.

Pfeffer, J. 1982. *Organizations and Organization Theory*. Boston, MA: Pittman.

Pfeffer, J. 1994. Competitive advantage through people. *California Management Review*, Winter 1994, 9–28.

Pfeffer, J. and Baron, J.N. 1988. Taking the workers back out: recent trends in the structuring of employment. *Research in Organizational Behavior*, 10: 257–303.

Podsakoff, P. and Organ, D. 1986. Self-reports in organizational research: problems and prospects. *Journal of Management*, 12: 531–544.

Polivka, A.E. and T. Nardone. 1989. On the definition of "contingent work." *Monthly Labor Review*, 112: 9–16.

Porter, M.E. 1980. *Competitive Strategy*. New York: Free Press.

Robinson, S.L., Kraatz, M.S. and Rousseau, D.M. 1994. Changing obligations and the psychological contract: a longitudinal study. *Academy of Management Journal*, 37: 137–152.

Rousseau, D.M. and Parks, J. McLean. 1993. The contracts of individuals and organizations. *Research in Organizational Behavior*, 15: 1–43.

Rousseau, D.M. and Wade-Benzoni, K.A. 1995. Changing individual-organizational attachments. In A. Howard (ed.) *Changing Nature of Work*. San Francisco: Jossey-Bass.

Schoonhoven, C.B. 1981. Problems with contingency theory: testing assumptions hidden within the language of contingency theory. *Administrative Science Quarterly*, 26: 349–377.

Segal, L.M. and Sullivan, D.G. 1995. The temporary labor force. *Economic Perspectives*, 19: March/April, 2–19.

Shapiro, A.C. 1989. *Modern Corporate Finance*. New York: Macmillan Publishing Company.

SHRM Alternative Staffing Survey 1998. Alexandria, VA: Society for Human Resource Management

Snell, S.A. 1992. Control theory in strategic human resource management: the mediating effect of administrative information. *Academy of Management Journal*, 35: 292–327.

Snell, S.A. and Dean, J.W., Jr. 1992. Integrated manufacturing and human resource management: a human capital perspective. *Academy of Management Journal*, 35: 467–504.

Sonnenfeld, J.A. and Peiperl, M.A. 1988. Staffing policy as a strategic response: a typology of career systems. *Academy of Management Review*, 13: 588–600.

Stone, E.F. and Hollenbeck, J.R. 1984. Some issues associated with the use of moderated regression. *Organizational Behavior and Human Performance*, 34: 195–213.

Tichy, N.M., Fombrun, C.J. and Devanna, M.A. 1982. Strategic human resource management. *Sloan Management Review*, Winter 1982, 47–61.

Ulrich, D., Yeung, A. and Brockbank, W. 1992. Developing multiple theoretical perspectives of strategic human resource management. Working paper, University of Michigan.

United States Equal Employment Opportunity Commission. 1994. *Job Classification Guide*. Washington, DC.

Venkatraman, N. 1989. The concept of fit in strategy research: toward verbal and statistical correspondence. *Academy of Management Review*, 14: 423–444.

Venkatraman, N. and Ramanujam, V. 1986. Measurement of business performance in strategy research: a comparison of approaches. *Academy of Management Review*, 11: 801–814.

Williamson, O.E. 1975. *Markets and Hierarchies: Analysis and Antitrust Implications*. New York: The Free Press.

Williamson, O.E. 1979. Transaction cost economics: the governance of contractual relations. *Journal of Law and Economics*, 22: 233–261.

Williamson, O.E. 1981. The economics of organization: the transaction cost approach. *American Journal of Sociology*, 87: 548–577.

Williamson, O.E. 1985. *The Economic Institutions of Capitalism*. New York: The Free Press.

Williamson, O.E. and Ouchi, W.G. 1981. The markets and hierarchies program of research: origins, implications, prospects. In A. Van de Ven and W.F. Joyce (eds.) *Perspectives on Organizational Design and Behavior*, 347–406. New York: John Wiley.

Woodward, J. 1965. *Industrial Organizations: Theory and Practice*. London: Oxford.

Woodward, J. 1970. *Industrial Organization: Behavior and Control*. London: Oxford.

Wright, P.M. and McMahan, G.C. 1992. Theoretical perspectives for strategic human resource management. *Journal of Management*, 18: 295–320.

Wright, P.M., Smart, D. and McMahan, G.C. 1995. On the integration of strategy and human resources: an investigation of the match between human resources and strategy among NCAA basketball teams. *Academy of Management Journal*, 38: 1052–1074.

Youndt, M.A., Snell, S.A., Dean, J.W. Jr. and Lepak, D.P. 1996. Human resource management, manufacturing strategy, and firm performance. *Academy of Management Journal*, 39: 836–866.

Author Index

Subject Index